P9-BHY-215

BREAKING
the Mother-Son
DYNAMIC

Redirecting the Patterns of a
Man's Life and Loves

JOHN LEE

Health Communications, Inc.
Deerfield Beach, Florida

www.hcibooks.com

CALGARY PUBLIC LIBRARY

MAR   2016

Library of Congress Cataloging-in-Publication Data
is available through the Library of Congress

© 2015 John Lee

ISBN-13: 978-07573-1866-5 (Paperback)
ISBN-10: 07573-1866-5 (Paperback)
ISBN-13: 978-07573-1867-2 (ePub)
ISBN-10: 07573-1867-3 (ePub)

All rights reserved. Printed in the United States of America. No part of this publica-
tion may be reproduced, stored in a retrieval system, or transmitted in any form or by
any means, electronic, mechanical, photocopying, recording, or otherwise, without the
written permission of the publisher.

HCI, its logos, and marks are trademarks of Health Communications, Inc.

Publisher: Health Communications, Inc.
      3201 S.W. 15th Street
      Deerfield Beach, FL 33442–8190

Cover design by Larissa Hise Henoch
Interior design and formatting by Lawna Patterson Oldfield

Dedicated to

Marjorie Sachs & Dan Miller

Also by John Lee

The Half-Lived Life: Overcoming Passivity and
Rediscovering Your Authentic Self

The Anger Solution: The Proven Method for Achieving Calm
and Developing Healthy, Long-Lasting Relationships

Growing Yourself Back Up: Understanding Emotional Regression

The Flying Boy: Healing the Wounded Man

The Flying Boy Book II: The Journey Continues

Facing the Fire: Experiencing and Expressing Anger Appropriately

Writing From the Body: For Writers, Artists, and
Dreamers Who Long to Free Their Voice

The Missing Peace: Solving the Anger Problem for Alcoholics,
Addicts, and Those Who Love Them

Emotional Intelligence for Couples: Simple Ways to Increase
the Communication in Your Relationship

The Secret Place of Thunder

Courting a Woman's Soul

When the Buddha Met Bubba

"When I was a boy, after my mother died, I always tried hard to hold her in my mind as I was falling asleep so maybe I'd dream of her, only I never did. Or, rather, I dreamed of her constantly, only as absence, not presence: a breeze blowing through a just-vacated house, her handwriting on a notepad, the smell of her perfume, streets in strange lost towns where I knew she'd been walking away only a moment before but had just vanished, a shadow moving away against a sunstruck wall. Sometimes I spotted her in a crowd, or in a taxicab pulling away, and these glimpses of her I treasured despite the fact that I was never able to catch up with her."

—*The Goldfinch*, Donna Tartt

"I never stopped praying for her," he says. "Never was there a time I didn't pray for her." . . . Jesus washed the feet of a beggar and forgave a whole world of sin; surely he would hear Jerry Lee pray for his mama."

—*Jerry Lee Lewis: His Own Story*, Rick Bragg

Contents

A Love Letter and Thank-You Note

There is no way to organize this by how much or how little each person or group contributed to this book.

Grace, you know who you are and that I love you. We are good friends and we worked to be so. No Grace, no book; it's as simple as that. You love well and deep.

Mary Norris, editor par excellence, your talent came shining through. You saw the life and love and (I'm happy to say) usefulness of the material in *Breaking the Mother-Son Dynamic*. Once again, I can't thank you enough for being such a delight to work with, as well as for your faith and friendship. Speaking of editors—my new editor at HCI, Allison Janse, has (as we say here in the Deep South) spit polished this project, so anything in it that shines is due to her talent and touch.

A very special thanks to you, Kat Hrdina, for coming into my life two years ago. You are the assistant every employer wants and tries to steal from another. Somehow, due to your extreme creative abilities (one being able to put up with me), you have become a major part of this project by adding, subtracting, and expanding so much. You have to be cited as assistant editor. This book wouldn't be what it is without your patience and love of the material, and through it all, you became my trusted confidant, counselor, and dear friend. Let's work on another one.

Marjorie Sachs, your response to this material in the webinar as a mother of two great young men inspired me to put this book into the hands of as many mothers, lovers, sons, and wives as I possibly can. A deep thank-you.

Thank you, Gary Seidler, for speaking with me at that conference in Arizona. You were so welcoming and supportive of me, bringing this project and myself back to HCI, my original publishing home.

Peter Vegso—God, we've known each other a long time. In many, many ways I owe you my career for believing in *The Flying Boy*. I appreciate your kind support of *Breaking the Mother-Son Dynamic* and hope it sells half as much as that old Flying book and that we keep our relationship alive and well, and I'll keep sending you book after book.

Thank you to all the folks at U.S. Journal Training and HCI: Dan Bartmueller, Suzanne Smith, Lorrie Keip, and Bob Ackerman.

Susan Lee, you're the best former wife a man can have. You've always believed in me and my writing, and while you didn't lend your talents to this particular book, your writing prowess and teaching make me a much better writer, if not husband. I love you, dear friend.

Bill Stott, your support over the years has been priceless, and I'll always owe you.

Dan Miller and Marjorie Sachs, thank you both for the love and support in many different ways to keep me going and writing. I'll never forget your kindness.

Finally, my gratitude goes out to Stacey Abel, a good writer and an old friend, for bringing just the right amount of light and energy while I was groping around in a dark place and wasn't sure if I had enough of either to see this project through. Thank you all!

—*John Lee*

Introduction

Breaking the Mother-Son Dynamic *has been written* with you in mind from the start, to help you view your relationship in non-shaming, non-blaming ways so you can clearly see, break, and dismantle what has become destructive. It provides men and women with fresh and sometimes frightening insights into the mysterious bond—or bondage—between millions of mothers and sons and how this bond impacts women as lovers, wives, and girlfriends.

The awareness of this dynamic will improve and perhaps change or save marriages, dating relationships, and the experience of living together, as well as increase the functionality of the family by showing everyone who is ready how to make a clean, clear, shame-free, guilt-free separation—to break free from unhealthy mothering and "sonning" that just hasn't worked. All of this will be a conscious, compassionate uncoupling of mothers and sons. Here comes the best part: I'm going to show you how to do the "work" and what the payoffs are for saying good-bye to Mom.

WHO THIS BOOK IS FOR

Breaking the Mother-Son Dynamic is for you if you are a son of any age who knows or feels that your relationship to your mother is not quite right. Thousands of men, old or young, can see that their relationships with their mothers have had a huge impact on how they relate to their lovers, wives, and girlfriends. In addition, the Mother-Son Dynamic also often negatively impacts sons' relationships to their fathers and may even result in a lack of or unsatisfying male friendships.

This book is for the man who wants to let his mother go and experience a healthy relationship with her as a separate adult. The women (or men if you are gay) you love don't want a "mama's boy"; they don't want a boy in men's clothing. Today's women want to know and feel that their lovers, husbands, or boyfriends always have their backs when push comes to shove, especially if his mother is doing the shoving. These strong women want men who are emotionally available, connected, and who are clearly comfortable with their masculinity, who won't be s/mothered, and who will still open up and let them in.

And for women: congratulations all you brave mothers of adult sons for being ready to stop seeing, treating, and thinking about your sons in ways that have been less than fruitful, less than correct, and perhaps even inappropriate! You are courageous enough to try to let your sons become the men they were meant to be and therefore treat women, wives, girlfriends, and lovers with respect and dignity and allow themselves to cherish and be cherished. All you have to do is let go. I'm going to show you how and, at the same time, show your sons how to compassionately let you go.

My compliments go to you proactive mothers who are raising sons with your eyes on their futures. You want to mother your sons in ways that feel right; you want to have boundaries and increase your sons' abilities in the future years to love and be loved in ways many of us older men had to learn through trial and error and broken hearts.

To the wives, girlfriends, lovers, and partners of men who may be caught up in this dynamic, I hope an understanding of how this happens will give you greater insight into your relationship. You, too, are perhaps suffering in a major or minor way because of this dynamic. By the end of this book, you'll gain knowledge, techniques, and tools for navigating and negotiating your relationship with both your husband, partner, or lover and his mother.

WHAT THIS BOOK PROMISES

In this book I provide both men and women with solutions, insights, stories, information, and tools that can turn relationships around, possibly even save some. I show men how to gently but assertively separate from what can be an overwhelming mother energy that has a massive magnetic pull on young and old men's hearts and souls. I teach women how to keep from being seen as a man's surrogate mother. I instruct well-meaning mothers how to stop acting in ways that minimize their sons' energy, even if they are doing it unknowingly or with no malicious intent.

Most of the men and women I have worked with (I include myself in this) thought as children that we were the reasons why our fathers or mothers drank, drugged, or beat us, or why they were emotionally or physically absent. Whatever was wrong in our families, we were to blame, causing us to be angry at our-selves instead of holding the adults in our lives accountable and responsible for their behavior. Even if we were ignored, left, or smothered with attention, we assigned ourselves accountability from childhood on. My young mother's life ran smack into my life when I was young, and she wrecked it with her smothering and abandoning. If I get angry at myself for this, I'll never heal, never trust other men or women, and will perpetuate the same behavior on to my children.

What I did, still do, and suggest to my clients and workshop par-ticipants is to assign accountability and take responsibility. Most of the time this is never done face-to-face but is done in the form of writing letters we do not send, fantasy dialoguing, sharing with a therapist, storytelling, creating, and other means.

I've worked with many people who are angry with themselves for many things. They don't know how to pray and they hold them-selves accountable for this instead of the ministers, preachers, and teachers whose job it is to teach them how to pray. There are angry fifty-year-olds who blame themselves because they "don't know how to do a relationship," as if they were supposed to be born with this information and skill. We do, we repeat, we parrot what was shown to us and what was taught to us until we get out from under the weight of holding ourselves accountable and then get respon-sible for educating ourselves about prayer, relationships, child rear-ing, learning how to love, being intimate, making love, and so on.

I invite you to join me on this journey, one that I have personally taken with my mother and the women in my life—from my wife to my sister, my niece, my grandniece—and tens of thousands of men and women who have shared their stories with me during the last thirty years as a counselor, therapist, workshop facilitator, and author. To maintain my integrity with my profession as a therapist and storyteller, I have changed the names, identifying characteristics, and certain locations and settings to protect the privacy and dignity of those whose stories I've told herein. With that said, everything in this work is true, or at least as true as memory will allow it to be.

If you are a man reading this, you may recognize some unresolved issues concerning how you were mothered. If you are a woman reading this, I hope you will see your husband, son, lover, or father on the following pages and come to a greater understanding of your relationship with him. And I hope both men and women alike will engage in the work that can lead to loving and living more fully and healthily.

DOING THE WORK

First, no kind of therapy, no counselors, and no self-help authors can make the good things a man or a woman has been taught go away. There's no way to remove the pleasant and positive from one's memory or heart. The work in this book, as indeed all my work with every client or workshop participant, is about healing the dysfunctional and being grateful for the kindness and love we received, wherever it came from. For example, my mother smothered me, and I can diminish and heal the negative repercussions of that. But she also taught me, among many other things, not to be racist, and that can never be diminished or taken away.

I trust that I have made it clear that consciousness has no room for blame. I believe that your mother—and mine—did the best she could with what she was given. If she didn't, I wouldn't be writing this and you couldn't be reading this. While I don't "blame" my mother, I do something in this book that has been taboo in this culture and others for too long: tell the truth about millions of mothers and sons and hold mothers accountable in the same way many have come to hold fathers accountable.

ACCOUNTABILITY, RESPONSIBILITY, AND BLAME

Webster's defines *accountability* as "liable to pay or make good in case of loss." Another definition is "the state of being accountable, liable, or answerable." *Responsibility*, says the dictionary, is being "able to respond to any claim, on one's own initiative or authority." Blame, however, is nothing like the other two. To blame is to "harass with constant criticism; to reproach for a lapse or misdeed."

Let me give an example. If I am driving down the road at the speed limit and I come to an intersection, see the light is green, and proceed through the intersection and a car zooms through the red light and runs into me and my car . . . who is accountable? The red-light runner, that's who. I'm going to get out of my car, shaken up a bit, probably a little scared and a little angry (if I'm not too much in shock) and ask the driver if he or she has insurance to pay for my damaged car, to make good in case of loss. I will hold the driver "accountable," and then I'll be "responsible" and take my car to the body shop to have it repaired. Conversely, if I held myself accountable for the driver's running the red light, I'd tell myself it was my fault for being in the wrong place at the wrong time and tell the red-light runner, "Oh, I'm so sorry I got in your line of fire. How silly of me to think I could drive down the road and expect others to obey the law. It's not necessary to contact your insurance agent, I'll pay for the damages—mine and yours—have a good day." Equally ridiculous is a reaction such as, "Look, you red-light runner, you come by my house tomorrow and pick up my damaged car and take it to the body shop; then go back and pick it up when it's fixed and bring it to me. In the meantime, give me the keys to your wife's car, which I'll be driving until you get mine fixed." We can agree on the most effective response: You ran into me, so you are accountable. I'll get the car fixed; I'm responsible for getting the repairs done.

Another way to think about this is that if a man carries the weight of both accountability and responsibility for his mother's misdeeds or mistakes, the two together will weigh him down and exhaust him so much that he'll be unlikely to have enough strength to handle both. Instead, he'll probably drink, drug, or get very depressed. By getting angry at what I call "The Ghost Mother"—not the one living today down in Florida but the one who was maybe too young to drive or be a mother—then I can carry the right weight of responsibility and take my wrecked car/life to the body shop/therapist and get it fixed. And since my mom didn't take out faulty-mother insurance, I'll have to be responsible for coming up with the money to have the work done. But I'm not accountable for the wreck. This story has a happy ending, but hold on! It gets a little bumpy, as any ride worth taking usually does.

Chapter 1

Recognizing the Mother-Son Dynamic

THE PRECISE DOSE OF A MOTHER'S LOVE,
PUNCTUALLY DELIVERED, IS THE CENTRAL
FACTOR IN THE WELL-BEING OF THE NEXT
GENERATION, THAT IS, THE FUTURE.

—*Shari Thurer*

A few years ago I spent seventy days facing fires I'd built to warm frozen memories and burn debris that cluttered my farm and my mind. I hadn't taken that much time off since before my best-selling book *The Flying Boy* was published. After that, between working and being on the road, I'd been able to keep my unseen psychic wounds stitched up most of the time. But during those seventy days, I came to realize I no longer wanted to keep my wounds sewn up. I pulled them open again, and when I did, I became terrified, energized, and depressed all at the same time.

Each day during that sabbatical I looked into blazing flames of my memories getting higher and higher. In the flickering flames, gradually the missing piece took shape—and the shape was my mother. In some inscrutable way, throughout my life I had been seeking the mothering I'd never had and desperately needed— seeking it in the faces and the embraces of many other women. I discovered increasing evidence that I was still tied to my mother in ways I'd denied for years. I also found myself smack-dab in the middle of a life crisis. And somehow, I knew the two were intimately linked.

The work I had done over the years had brought me ever closer to healing the wounds I'd received from my father. But something my mother took from me, or should have given me as a child, was out there somewhere: behind the flames, in my mother's kitchen, in my partner's approval, in the faces of workshop participants, on the desk of my publisher, in the darkness at three in the morning. I needed to find this part of myself and reclaim it. But how?

I set out to write a very different book from the one you're holding in your hands. I wanted to write about how the proceeds from my first three books would allow Grace, my former partner and lover, and me to buy a farm in the paradisiacal Blue Ridge Mountains and return to my Southern roots. I'd tell you how Grace and I were raising sheep, horses, vegetables, and a baby; that we had stepped into the mystery of matrimony and solved it; that we had a few difficulties but generally were living happily ever after; and that you probably wouldn't be hearing from me again.

So much for the best-laid plans. Want to make God laugh? Tell him your plans. So goes the joke.

A VISIT FROM MOTHER

About a month after we moved to Asheville, North Carolina, my mother visited. She told me two separate but related things that changed me and, thus, the direction of this book and my life.

She told me the first thing she thought after reading my first book, *The Flying Boy*, was "How come he didn't write anything about me?" Later, after reading my book *At My Father's Wedding*, she saw that I'd made a deep and final peace with my father—a peace I had yet to make with her. I was stunned by her astute observation, so stunned that at first I denied it. I thought I'd done all the "mother work" I needed to do in this lifetime. Months passed before I was ready to admit she was right.

During that year on the farm, I discovered that my partner, Grace, reminded me more of my mother than I can say without cursing. I now think of the farm as the Cauldron, because it was a container for a vast, hot, swirling stew of feelings, experiences, memories, pain, and joy. Then I found a great therapist nearby, a Virgil to my Dante, who guided me through therapy hell for two years. In the process I discovered more about how my mother was in reality—and how much I wanted the idealized mother I'd never had. This desire had wrapped me like a burial shroud or, more accurately, like a layer of plastic wrap preserving me, allowing others to see me but never quite touch me and keeping me from touching them.

On the farm, that Cauldron, I could not escape the heat generated by my relationship with Grace. There we worked together all day and night, and played together sometimes. Over the months we watched every pattern we had each used to survive childhood come out and try to destroy us.

Being in this relationship pot brought out one of my worst patterns: being critical. It seemed that nothing Grace did pleased me, and I let her know it through scorching words. In time I saw that this pattern was part of my legacy from my father. He too was overly critical. My mother had devoted her energies to trying to please him. As I interpreted it, she filled his plate by giving him everything from her own. That left her with little to give to me and my younger brother and sister.

I watched as Grace let my criticism wash over her, sink into her, and dissolve some of her youth, energy, and passion. Watching myself do this to her was more painful than I could stand. Sometimes I thought about leaving her just so I could stop being hurtful to the one I loved so much. How does the old song go? "Why Do We Always Hurt the Ones We Love?" Soon, though, Grace built a dam of anger to protect herself from my flood of critical words. Her strength helped both of us. In time I was forced to see that I would have to deal with the half-empty plate my mother gave me if I were ever to come to terms with the anger I (and many other men) have misdirected at women for not meeting my needs.

The second thing my mother told me during this visit made me numb for months. It happened one day when we walked out into the meditation garden and sat on the bench overlooking the lake. Slowly she opened up and began talking about how my father had physically abused me when I was fourteen months old. I had already dealt with the hurt and grief over later beatings. I felt I had done so much work concerning the abuse I received from my father that, in a way, this was just more of the same stuff I'd known for a long time. But suddenly, Mom burst into tears. "I didn't stop him," she sobbed, saying this over and over. Finally she said how sorry she was and that she wanted to make amends. She asked my forgiveness.

My mother was admitting that she had been unable—or unwilling—to protect me in my most vulnerable time. Yet, as I grew older, this same woman had expected me to protect her from my father's onslaughts. I had supported her, when I, the child, should have been protected and provided for by her. Beginning at the tender age of five, I listened to her pain, brought her cool cloths for her migraines, and tried to counsel her. I knew then and there that my feelings of distrust for women had begun with my mother, the first and most important woman in my life. My shock at realizing this was so great that rather than process my troubling feelings, I was thrown into a deep depression.

These two utterances from my mother changed me forever. I knew as I journeyed back into my history with my mother that I would have to go through all my feelings about her and her lack of mothering that were buried inside my bones, my body, and my brain. I knew I'd have to re-experience fully how I'd been affected by having my body beaten and my energy robbed. I would have to deal with the pattern of always finding "mothers" to take care of, and then trying to get them to take care of me. I would have to grieve that I had never been as close to another person as I'd yearned to be, never really allowed anybody in.

HOW PARADISE WAS LOST

I knew that instead of writing a book about Paradise found, I would have to deal with how Paradise was lost in the first place. I'd write a book about sons and mothers that paralleled the work I had done about sons and fathers. I would relate my personal story to the stories of other men's lives and their loving and letting go of the mothers who live in our memories, dreams, and fantasies. I'd regain some sense of wholeness this way, come full circle, and increase my ability for intimacy in the process. I would connect past to present and hope that I came out healthier than when I went in.

Many moments over the years—while writing, sometimes while giving a talk, or after staying alone in the woods for a week—I felt whole and content. But I could never hold on to the feeling of wholeness. In the same way, I remember as a boy being unable to hold on to my mother except for short moments. The missing part of me that my mother withheld when I was a child finds its way back to me occasionally, but it soon disappears, coming and going according to its whim. At first I wasn't sure what this meant, but I was sure of this: my biological mother disappeared into the night. After I was one or two years old, she no longer came when I needed her.

I didn't know what I wanted to do next: write another book, try to write a screenplay, get off the road and return to teaching, buy a '65 Mustang convertible, or give up everything for a twenty-five-year-old blonde, brunette, or redhead. Sometimes my thoughts made me feel embarrassed and ashamed. Here I was, author of numerous books, publisher of a magazine, founder of the Austin Men's Center, and owner of a wonderful farm in the mountains of North Carolina. I was moving into my third year with Grace. After all my years of therapy and recovery, how could I be thinking about sleek cars and twenty-five-year-olds? It was a classic life crisis.

As I looked into the fire, I felt a deep ache rise up in me, as though the flames were burning away parts of my soul. I was afraid to keep still, afraid that if I didn't get back to work soon there'd be no soul at all left in me—only ashes. But I kept sitting and staring. Perhaps if I looked long enough, the flames would reveal what I felt to be missing inside me. I wasn't sure what that part was or what to call it. I just sensed it was missing. I remembered a poem from the Spanish poet, Antonio Machado: "I thought my fire was out, and stirred the ashes. I burned my fingers."

I share my personal story about my own mothering to show the value of recognizing it in your current (and previous) adult relationships. I want to be clear again that it need not involve shame or blame, just honesty about the way you feel. I hope my example will give you the encouragement and tools to face your own Mother-Son Dynamic and become the separate, adult son that you are, or to become a mother who encourages this appropriate, healthy separation with your son. Along with my story, you will encounter exercises that will allow you to join in the conversation and, at the same time, examine your own story. I've included these exercises, tools, techniques, and information for mothers, for sons, and for wives, girlfriends, and partners of adult sons where appropriate.

Exercise for Sons

A man must, in a healthy manner, express and feel anger toward and grieve the mother he wanted and never had, or the mother he had and never wanted. Perhaps your mother was not as active and engaging as you wanted her to be, or she may have been too engaged and diverted by many other things that she gave attention to someone other than you. Perhaps she was a socialite and you wanted a stay-at-home mom. Maybe she was not very educated and couldn't discuss with you the things that interested you. Possibly she was cold and you needed a great deal of warmth. These are some things you might want to consider. Remember, we're not trying to shame her or blame her. We are trying to balance your skewed view of the mother you were dealt so you can see her as the person she was or is and to see yourself as you are.

The following exercise is designed to help you explore your relationship to your mother while still being respectful and appreciative of who your mother was and possibly still is. It is designed to help you get in touch with feelings of sadness and maybe some anger. Try to be as honest as possible, letting emotions come out freely.

Draw a vertical line down the center of a piece of paper and on one side write "Attributes" and on the other "Deficiencies." List your mother's attributes, which may range from the hugs and affection she gave to the opportunities she provided for you. Include anything you feel truly supported your best interests and is benefiting you in your adult life. Next, list her deficiencies, which may be emotional or physical and are likely to include things you needed but she couldn't or didn't provide for you.

Don't worry about how it may sound; your mother will not see this list, since you're doing it privately on your notepad or computer. Best case, you will see a more balanced person than an idealized icon. If your mother happens to still be alive, this balanced view will increase the possibility of a more objective and compassionate relationship all the way around. Remember, one of the primary goals of this book is to help you see your mother through adult eyes, thus allowing you to see the woman or women in your life as they really are rather than as surrogate mothers. Anthony De Mello says, "How can you love someone whom you do not even see?"

This first exercise may be the most difficult, since you may be just starting the process of seeing your mother as a separate human being, with her own set of challenges and shortcomings as well as virtues. As you move forward in examining your relationship with your mother, keep this list nearby. It will serve as a building block for your work in some of the coming exercises. You may even choose to add to it as you read further in this book and begin to see more clearly what role mothers can play in our lives.

Here's another exercise sons will find useful. Write a letter to your mother (not to send) telling her how you were mothered and how you weren't. Tell her in this letter (which you will burn) what you needed and didn't get, what you got and didn't need. Tell her how her style of mothering impacted and shaped your life.

GOING HOME AGAIN

Thomas Wolfe said, "You can never go home again." However, to go forward, I have to go backward from time to time. I return to the places where the dreams began: my hometown and the small college where I did my undergraduate work. That's where I'm sitting right now, writing these pages. Through the windows I see the amphitheater where I used to sit on hard green benches daydreaming of being a writer. I try looking outward for any part of me that might still be sitting on one of these benches or walking among the eternally young, hoping that an outward sight will trigger an inner version of myself. Today I need to see a familiar face from my past, someone who knew me when I hid my face behind beer cans, marijuana smoke, and Southern stoicism. Although I spot people I think I recognize, they simply resemble someone I used to know. The "me" I imagine I see is not the "me" I am now. But who am I, now separate from the mother who birthed me and merged with me? I've always been looking for clues that could help shed some light on the blacked-out memory of my childhood. Now at this point it seems even more necessary. So I wander back to my childhood home and play the role of a Southern Sherlock Holmes, trying to discover my true identity. What I come up with is an identity made up of a patchwork of many former selves: the murderer of time, the thief of hearts, the depressed preacher, the drinker of cheap wine and beer, the perpetual worrier and wanderer, the would-be writer, the likable guy who almost never uttered the word *no* to his mother or anyone else except myself.

I know and feel at some level that the Mother is the matrix of our existence. *Matrix*, in fact, means "womb." Our biological mothers are the entrance to the Great Mystery in all its different forms and guises. It is the Mother who makes Oedipus first a son, then a lover and husband, and finally a blind man. It is the Mother who makes Parsifal a hero, yet who keeps him from taking a wife. (I'll have more to say about Parsifal and his search for the Holy Grail later.) It is the Mother who keeps some men from fully giving themselves over to women they love.

Men must acknowledge these facts if they hope to separate from their mothers. They must recognize, too, how they turn women into mothers and how they often play mother to others as a way of increasing their sense of self-worth. I choose my childhood home, my mother's country home, because the Great Return is back to the mother from whom we came.

Today I am visiting my hometown of Tuscumbia, Alabama. During lunch in a small café, I hear a good example of how the mother stays with a man no matter how old he is. A waiter, whom I judged to be in his early thirties, was talking to three women. It was after the lunch crowd had left, so he could relax and enjoy the everybody-knows-everybody-and-nobody's-in-a-rush way of a small town. I listened a bit to their conversation, amused that even though I hadn't lived here in thirty years, I still knew a lot about some of the people and places they were discussing.

At one point my ears perked up. The young man said that he had recently played a role in a local production of a Neil Simon play. "I had to curse several times in the play," he said. "When my mother was in the audience, I was terrified. She'd never heard me talk like that."

I dropped out of their talk for a moment to place my order. When I tuned in again I heard him say: "I'm a big Monty Python fan. They did a great take-off on Christianity in *The Life of Brian*, and they were wonderfully sacrilegious in *Monty Python and the Holy Grail*. My mother wouldn't allow me to see either one when they first came out. To this day I don't dare tell her they're some of my favorites—I can't tell her I've even seen these movies."

As I sipped my coffee, I began to wonder. Was this young man showing respect for his mother? Did the women listening to him admire and respect him for being such a good son, a "good little boy"?

I hear adult sons say all the time that they'd like to tell their mothers all kinds of things. When asked why they don't, they reply: "It wouldn't do any good." "It would upset her too much." "It would just kill her." The son who was raised solely or mostly by the mother comes to believe that the power she has over him is immense and also has an exaggerated sense of power to impact—for better or for worse—her life. He is always editing, censoring, and hiding parts of himself out of fear of what he thinks she'll think.

The reluctance to show our real selves to our mothers is reflected in a popular TV commercial. A thirtysomething man has just poured himself a bowl of cereal when his mom calls him on the phone. He's afraid of two things: one, his cereal is going to get soggy (it won't—that's the point of the commercial); and, two, he'll have to tell his mother he can't talk to her right then. He goes through all kinds of physical contortions trying to eat his cereal, never quite succeeding. Finally it hits him: he pulls the table over to the phone and hooks the phone to the table, mouthpiece up. Delighting in his ingenuity—and his crisp cereal—he continues eating, occasionally muttering, "Yeah, Ma, uh-huh . . ." into the phone, without hearing a word she says.

An ancient example of Mother's perpetual influence comes to us from the myth of the Holy Grail. In his important book *He*, Robert Johnson does a masterful job of illuminating and interpreting this myth. The Grail, as Johnson says, is the "great cornucopia of life." It pours out its abundance and blessings on humankind. The one who finds it is Parsifal, whose name means "innocent fool."

Parsifal is born to a woman named Heart's Sorrow. Parsifal's father is absent, and he is raised by his mother. As Johnson points out, "The redeeming hero in mythology often has no father and is raised in humble and lonely circumstances." Heart's Sorrow keeps the boy with her, always fearful that someday he'll want to be a knight like his father and brothers before him, and she'll be left alone. One day Parsifal sees five knights in full armor and is so impressed that he decides to join them. His mother bursts into tears, realizing she has failed to keep her son from discovering the ways of men.

How many men today have seen these knights and felt a similar longing? These "knights," Johnson says, might have appeared in the form of a football hero, a poet, a doctor, a movie star, or a telephone lineman. When we saw them we thought, "I would dearly love to go and become a rider [or a writer, a star, or a lineman]. But I would have to leave my mother behind, and she depends on me. So I'll take a job at the local factory instead. I'll move into a house just down the road. I'll come up every evening to check on her, and we'll have dinner together every Sunday until we die."

Unable to hold Parsifal any longer, Heart's Sorrow lets him go. But before he leaves she gives him a garment she has woven for him. The garment is very fine and lightweight, in contrast to the heavy, male, masculine armor he will soon wear over it. I believe the homespun garment symbolizes the Mother's overprotection, while the armor symbolizes the Father's abandonment. Together they insulate a man from the world around him. As long as we wear these things, we men remain disconnected, distant from those we wish to be close to, and less creative than we're meant to be. The homespun garment plays an important part in the boy's adventure because it symbolizes not only his need to please his mother but later his guilt at leaving.

Parsifal hasn't had a father, an older brother, or uncles to instruct him in the secrets vital to manhood. All he has is his mother's teachings and wisdom—useful, but not complete. He meets maidens and challenges other knights, but he doesn't know what he's doing until he meets his mentor: Gournamond. This older male figure teaches him two very important things: 1) he must never seduce or be seduced by a fair maiden, and 2) he must search for the Grail Castle with all his might. Johnson makes it clear these injunctions should not be taken literally; in psychological terms they refer to Parsifal's inner world. The "maiden" is the interior feminine, or anima, as Jung calls it, and the castle is Parsifal's "kingdom within."

When Parsifal left, his mother instructed him "not to ask too many questions." Compare this with the teaching of Gournamond, who tells Parsifal that when he finds this wonderful castle, he is to ask the most important question a man or woman will ever ask: "Whom does the Grail serve?"

Yet as soon as Gournamond gives him these instructions, Parsifal suddenly remembers his mother and goes in search of her again, only to find that shortly after he left she died of a broken heart. We always remember our moms just before we do something they wouldn't approve of.

Similarly, many men think about and miss their wives or lovers as soon as they get into a "men-only" situation. I remember one young man who left a men's weekend retreat the first day, saying, "The way for me to do good as a man is to be with my girlfriend." (See *At My Father's Wedding: Reclaiming Our True Masculinity*.) Another man I know was always afraid to tell his mother he wasn't coming home for Christmas because he thought "it would break her heart." So he and his wife would defer their dream of enjoying Christmas in the Bahamas because of his mother, who might just as well be named Heart's Sorrow.

Every man must separate from his mother—or else he will carry his mother with him out into the world. Men who don't separate never quite attain their masculinity. I had a dream a few nights ago in which my mother told me I was disappointing someone by not going to his city to give a lecture. I said in the dream, "To hell with them! I have to take care of myself first!" In shock, she replied, "You have never said that to me."

And it was true. Only recently have I learned to tell my mother no. The other day my mother called to ask me for a loan to help her buy a house. I had to refuse. I simply did not have money to lend her. But had she asked even a year or two before, I would have volunteered to get the money somehow rather than say no to her.

In certain primitive cultures, the boy is taken from the force field of women through symbolic rituals and acts. Sometimes this takes place in the form of mock abductions. The women collude with the men and everything is arranged beforehand. During the ritual the boy is snatched from his mother by the male elders. The women of the village make a big fuss and try to keep the men from taking him. This shows the boy that he is important to them and that they don't want to see him go any more than Heart's Sorrow wanted Parsifal to go. But, as prearranged, the men win the struggle and take the boy off for several days of fasting and instruction.

If a boy grows up without experiencing this separation from the world of mothers, ritually or otherwise, his capacity for relationships with women will be diminished. He will remain in the grip of the mother, letting her carry his feminine side for him rather than being given the chance to discover it for himself. He will then have a tendency to let every flesh-and-blood woman he loves carry his feminine for him.

When the romance is over, when the blinders he unconsciously wears during courtship are removed by the reality of day-to-day living, he will discover that this woman has a soul, a being of her own. He will see that she is not, in fact, his mother, and he will become hostile and distant. He won't be able to articulate why this is happening, but he will sense that something is missing or has been stolen from him, and that this woman has it. In truth she possesses nothing he doesn't have; he just has yet to discover this fact and to find in himself what he feels to be missing.

The following lists for sons and mothers have been composed of some of the nonscientific but real clues I've gained after working with men and women for thirty years, as well as from my own experience. They're designed to help you determine if the Mother-Son Dynamic is in play in your relationships.

Exercise for Sons

1. If your partner, wife, or girlfriend (or male lover) is in an argument or heated discussion with your mother, do you find yourself taking your mother's side, or hear from your significant other that you repeatedly do so?

2. Do you still hold back, swallow, or bottle up things you wish you could have said to your mother for fear it would upset or "kill" her?

3. Do you feel tension between you and your father when your mother is present?

4. Do you ever feel, if push came to shove, that your mother would choose you over her husband, your father, or your stepfather?

5. Did you grow up hearing negative things about "men," "masculinity," "being a male," and that your mother didn't want you to be like the rest of men?

6. Have you made radical changes like moving, quitting a good job, or leaving a relationship to be closer to your mother?

7. How far do you live from your mother now, or have you for most of your adult life?

    a. Two blocks

    b. Two miles

    c. A thousand or more miles

    d. In the room you had as a kid

    e. In her basement

8. Does your mother, or did she, respect your boundaries as a child, adolescent, or adult?

9. Does your mother, or did she, get a little too affectionate, especially after taking too much alcohol or drugs, or even without?

10. Does your mother, or did she, refer to you as her "baby" or "her little boy" even after you became an adult?

If you answered yes to at least several of these questions, you would benefit from doing the work described in this book.

Exercise for Mothers

The following are statements that men have told me in sessions, workshops, and conferences that their mothers have said to them. They are common phrases that enmeshed, over-attached mothers have said to their sons (particularly grown sons). These are said with the best of intentions, without an awareness of the potentially detrimental impact. Throughout the book we'll learn more positive ways to interact with a grown son; but for now, try to identify if you say or have said these things to your adolescent or adult son:

- "No one will ever love you as much as I do."
- "You will always be my 'little boy,' 'baby,' 'hero.'"
- "Beware of women; they only want you for your money."
- "You can always come home; I'll keep your room just as you left it."
- "There's no one in the world you can trust except me."
- "Now if you don't stay in touch, it will break my heart."

Exercise for Mothers and Sons

The following are reasons why a mother may enmesh or be caught in an unhealthy Mother-Son Dynamic. Both mothers and sons should determine if any of these apply in your situation:

- Someone merged or enmeshed with her, probably in childhood.
- Someone abandoned her, probably in childhood.
- She didn't have any sense of self.
- She didn't have good, or any, boundaries.
- She was left alone due to death, divorce, or disease.
- She was mentally unstable.
- She didn't really love or commit to her husband.

- She was addicted to work, alcohol, drugs, television, gambling, the computer, sex, or something else.

- She was physically exhausted, and her son soothed her instead of vice versa.

- She subjugated her power and looked to her son to live through him vicariously.

- She wanted her son to rescue her, heal her and the family.

- She didn't know the difference or error of emotional incest versus sexual incest.

WRESTLING WITH THE WITCH

*And it's right that the grown man
shivers and remains silent.*

—Rilke

The other night I had a dream: I was running down a dark street. I had a lot of money in my wallet and knew it was dangerous to be in that part of the city. Some young gang members started running beside me. I was afraid they would hurt me. I ran faster but found them to be completely uninterested in me or my money. Suddenly I found myself on the front porch of a house. A hideously ugly, unkempt woman appeared, speaking horrible words and snatching at my money. I managed to escape. But I knew I hadn't "wrestled" with her and won. I had merely run away. Something told me I would have to face her again in the future.

In dreams and fairy tales, as in life, Man wants Woman—beautiful, sensuous, desirable Woman. He runs away from the "ugly sister" or the "hideous damsel" or the "witch" who appears in fairy tales and dreams, often as a princess. Yet many old tales feature scenes in which a young man must embrace the less than attractive, usually aging woman as part of his rite of passage into manhood. He must not be afraid of her grotesqueness or the possible power she may possess. Disney's version of *Beauty and the Beast* opens with just such a scene; because the prince shuns the hag, she turns him into a grotesque monster.

For men, the source of this aversion to the witch is usually the relationship to Mother. Try as they may to repress the witch within, many mothers eventually reveal that side of themselves. We see it in the resentful, aging mother who envies her son's first date and eventually his young wife. Many mothers try to hide this, putting their best foot forward, looking their best, bestowing loving smiles all around. But then they feel a craving to eat their young children, much as many mothers have nibbled on their babies' toes while saying, "I could just eat Mama's little darling up."

In her dissertation *Medusa's Daughters: A Study of Women's Consciousness in Myth and Poetry*, Karen Elias-Button writes:

> The Great Mother's maternal force has often been characterized as grasping, even paralyzing, its effect sometimes damaging. . . . This dark side of the "mother," whose face is Medusa's own, has found its way into male mythology and psychology as . . . the Stone Mother . . . whose powers must be permanently destroyed to enable the male "hero" to attain maturity.

This witch, or Stone Mother, existed in everybody's mothers except our own—or so we may have thought as children. By late adolescence and early adulthood, we knew how terrible our mothers could sometimes be, but we dared not let that knowledge seep into our consciousness and certainly not into our language. Our mothers were always shining paragons of virtue, idols whose images we would suffer no one to sully. If we got into fights, we knew that insulting the other person's mother was the quickest, surest way to provoke him. "Your mother wears army boots!" was one of the milder expressions of bygone days; a more vivid insult appears in the movie *The Exorcist* when the devil tries to anger the priest by saying, "Your mother sucks cocks in hell!" And in Spike Lee's *Malcolm X*, a man tries every way he knows to rile Malcolm and finally succeeds when he says something about his mother— so Malcolm smashes a beer bottle over his head.

Trying to hold on to an image of Mother as all-good is natural. But the darkness inside Mother must also be made part of our conscious awareness. If not, then we push the witch into the dungeon of our unconscious, where it is at risk of being projected onto flesh-and-blood women who at worst we burn at the stake and at best we simply ignore. Sometimes the all-bad witch-Mother is the dominant image a man carries through life. If this witch resides in the forefront of his consciousness, he becomes witchy himself: sarcastic, critical, perfectionistic, envious, or jealous—all of it witchy and hideous.

Until a man can admit to himself that his mother isn't all sweetness and light, he will carry the witch inside him, refusing to embrace her or to wrestle with her. He will never acknowledge that he not only loves his mother but hates her as well. He will never be whole. If men don't wrestle with the witch in their mothers, when the witch in their wives or lovers needs confronting, they won't do it. Instead comes the passive-aggressive "Whatever you say, dear."

And that witch will eat him alive. And an easy job she'll have of it too, because there will be no bones—particularly backbone—for her to break her teeth on.

But as the fairy tales would have us understand, the act of embracing the witch sometimes transforms her into a wise old woman, known as a crone, who is more willing than we ever guessed to guide us to the interior princess. After all, the witch has special powers; she knows the way through the dark forest that separates us from another part of ourselves.

Once when my mother came to visit Grace and me at the farm in Asheville, she decided to let her worst side, the hideous witch, be fully present during the visit. She was controlling and passive-aggressive. At times she seemed ready to throw me into a boiling pot on the stove.

I realized that I had never fully let myself see this side of my mother. I always thought of her in the way that most people think of her: a loving, funny, charming Christian lady. But when raising us, she sucked out my energy to fill her own life and I became her surrogate husband because my father was absent. But I had not, somehow, put the responsibility of this on her. I had carefully explored my father in my writings, listing his many failings, analyzing our relationship closely and, I realized now, unconsciously blaming him for making my mother turn me into a man before my time. Maybe if he hadn't been absent (so my thinking went), that never would have happened.

But during this visit to our farm, I knew that the time had come at last to face the witch in my mother. She knew it, too; as I said earlier, Mom was well along in her recovery, and she had pointed out that I hadn't yet found peace with her in the way I had with my father.

The wrestling match began. I confronted her about the controlling, manipulative behavior I'd experienced from her the day, and decades, before. It was not a pretty sight. She yelled. I yelled. She got up to walk out but then sat back down. She verbally attacked me, and then listened to me, heard me, and loved me. Finally we embraced. It was amazing. Both of us were aware that I had never spoken to her that way, face-to-face, in my life. In contrast to my usual non-confrontational way of being, I realized that in the last several months I'd been in two other rather ugly, unpleasant but highly energizing shouting matches with a couple of women—Grace and my mom. During those episodes I hadn't really cared whether those women thought I was a "nice guy" or not. They certainly didn't think that—and, lo and behold, I didn't die.

After we cooled off from our confrontation, Mom told me that when she was my age, she had wrestled with the witch in her mother. She had told her that she had never felt loved by her. The same kind of exchange had resulted: anger, tears, and words flowed out of them for nearly a full day. After that my mother felt loved by her mother. Interestingly, Mom said that although she had never raised her voice to her mother before that day, she did so many times in the years to come. They argued, fought, and confronted each other—and as a result my mom felt seen, heard, and loved.

Facing the witch breaks loose a whole new kind of energy in a relationship, and it often ends up bringing people closer. A colleague of mine has said many times that he can't trust anyone he can't fight with. I'm beginning to understand what he means.

Men, you can do this even if your mother has died; you just have to be able to articulate her witchiness. The payoff for fully understanding a relationship with a mother who has already passed on is as great as if she were still alive. Much of the work in breaking the Mother-Son Dynamic is not going to lead a man to directly confront his mother. This work is to be done in journal writing or creativity of any kind, talking with the men in your men's group, writing letters that will never be sent, and so on.

Exercise for Sons

Here you're going to try facing the witch in your mother, knowing that this is only one aspect of the complete person she is. The goal is to get in touch with the things you may be feeling but have not previously admitted to yourself or anyone else, let alone your mother.

- Imagine you are in the same room with her and can tell her anything that is on your mind or in your heart, even things you feel would hurt her. You may want to state these gently; perhaps you will want to yell and scream. Both are absolutely fine, since there is no wrong way to do this. If possible, do this when and where you can express yourself out loud in private. Remember, you won't be confronting your mother in the flesh; what you say in this exercise will not hurt her.

- What things would you like to tell your mother about how you were raised and about your current relationship with her?

- How do you feel when you say these things out loud?

- If this exercise is too difficult, I suggest you take pen and paper, or type on your computer, and write these things out, being as truthful as you can. These pages are meant to be seen by you alone, unless or until you would like to share them.

I highly recommend not actually confronting your mother in person until you have completed the work in this book and have a deeper understanding of yourself and the relationship you share. Right now, we are gathering information and learning. Before I confronted my mother in person about this, I had done intense therapy work, which I'll relate to you in Chapter 4. During this anger work with a therapist, I discharged a lot of pent-up anger before I ever confronted my mother for the first time, and that's what I suggest you and all my clients, male and female, do.

Exercise for Mothers

Motherhood is an extremely complex undertaking, and almost every mother has the best intentions for her child's welfare—which is probably one of the main reasons you mothers have picked up this book. Remember, you are a complex human being in a complex role, and examining all these parts of yourself in this role can give you a better understanding of it and lead to the healthiest parenting behaviors possible. Later in the book, I'll share more about the witch in ourselves that we all (men and women alike) benefit from encountering.

- Do you feel a witchiness in yourself? Do you feel any darkness in yourself regarding your son, any areas in which you may have been too little or too much in a certain aspect of his life when he was a child? How about as an adult?

- Did you witness any witchy behavior in your mother that you have repeated with your son or your husband?

- Write a letter to your son, articulating how you are trying or have tried to mother him. Do you realize any things you couldn't or didn't give, or gave too much of? Do you still find yourself trying to compensate for them? Can you see if it shaped his life in ways you intended or didn't intend?

After a deep letting go of pent-up feelings in a safe and appropriate way, there may come a time when it would feel right, as it did for my mother and me, to speak directly about these things. If the work has been done by both mother and son, a conversation like this will probably not last more than thirty minutes to an hour.

LOSS OF THE BIOLOGICAL MOTHER

I want to describe myself like a painting
I looked at closely for a long time,
like a saying that finally understood,
like the pitcher I use every day,
like the face of my mother.

—Rilke

Most men today know little about their births. To deal with the kind of mothering we received—or didn't receive—we must go back to the moment we came into this world. Several years ago, I called my mother and asked her to tell me about the day I was born. I wanted all the information she had so I could feel that knowledge down to my bones.

The words she spoke stung my soul and at the same time confirmed some deep-rooted suspicions. She told me that her labor had been excruciating. She suffered for twenty-four hours before the doctors finally anesthetized her pain—and me—away. When I emerged, I encountered men and women hidden behind masks. A bright light shone in my half-blind, half-open eyes.

At that time, the whole experience of childbirth was viewed largely as a surgical procedure rather than an act of nature. Men and women wore gowns and gloves; machinery moved toward me and then away. Smells, foreign and unfriendly, penetrated my nose. My mother was in pain. I was whisked from her womb, wrapped in a cloth rather than her arms, and removed to sterile quarters for many hours before I had any contact with her, and then it was for only a few moments. Were this style of birth the exception to the rule, it would not be worth recounting here. But it was not. We humans are the only animal that allows our infants to be pulled away before some form of bonding or imprinting—nuzzling, smelling, licking, snuggling—has occurred. As Dr. Anthony Stevens says, "Loss or absence of mother . . . means more to the stricken infant than loss of someone to care for his bodily needs." When my mom told me this story of my birth day, I felt my loss—our losses, hers and mine—and I wept with sadness.

Whatever the scientists and sociologists may tell us, I cannot help but believe that after our births, it's best if we can be placed on our mothers' chests, still tied by the umbilical cord, still wet, still crimson, more fluid than form, more fantasy than fact. Today, many births are carried out this way, thank goodness.

I also believe that because of the way many of us arrived in the world, our social and survival skills are damaged. Many of us have an "attachment disorder." Only with time, therapy, and grieving can we heal ourselves. We need to become parents who don't treat children as if they were inanimate objects or extensions of ourselves. We need to become capable of true, healthy attachment rather than enmeshed and dependent relationships. Until men work at healing their dependency on their children, we'll keep cycling through the predictable sequence of behavior that the psychologist John Bowlby describes in his work on attachment. The sequence has three phases: protest, despair, detachment. In the protest phase, the baby cries and screams for the mother, doesn't sleep, throws itself about, shakes its crib, and does everything it can to bring the mother back.

We men who experienced losing our mothers, whether for a short time or for long periods, also physicalize our loss. We look distressed—furrowed brow, intense expression, sad eyes, a mask of hopelessness and despair (what I call the "flying boy" look)— even though we may be only twentysomething. To compensate, we try with all our might to turn our lovers into the mothers we lost. We still need our mothers so much that we refuse to believe they ever left us in the first place. Think about all the times when someone—not you—decided to break off a relationship. Didn't you go through an excruciating time when you believed with all your heart and soul that that person would come back, or if only they would come back, the hole in your heart would be filled?

The second phase, according to Bowlby, is despair. Now the child is preoccupied with his missing mother but feels increasingly hopeless. The physical movements of protest diminish or stop. He may cry monotonously off and on, and gradually he becomes withdrawn. I'm sure that when I was a six-hour-old infant who couldn't find his mother within the tiny universe of my touch, I became depressed. I was to experience that feeling again and again as my mother popped in and out of my life according to the dictates of her needs—not mine.

Similarly, the man who longs for mothering and doesn't get it becomes depressed. I have worked with many men—and women for that matter—who are deep inside this second phase. I hear it in their voices—the resignation, the hopelessness. When telling their stories, if they do get any tears out at all, they cry monotonously or off and on. They don't have the full-body cries of a child who still has hope that his mother will return.

The third phase is detachment. In some ways this is the most critical phase for the infant as well as for the adult child. In this stage a child shows more interest in his surroundings than in his mother. If the mother appears, he may remain remote and apathetic to her. As Bowlby wrote, "Instead of tears there is a listless turning away. He seems to have lost all interest in her." This child becomes self-centered. Instead of getting close to people and letting people get close to him, he "will become preoccupied with natural things such as sweets, toys, and food . . . he no longer appears to care for anyone." This boy grows into a man who favors objects, collecting more and more material possessions. He will also treat people as objects and find it difficult to develop deep and lasting relationships, even with his children. It's as if he draws sustenance from things he accumulates. The fear of not accumulating them causes him more despair than the thought of not having a wife or a family to come home to at the end of a hard day. This man may also be the type who selects his wife to complement his home, car, and stereo, the man whose children are testaments to his ability to extract from the earth all the possessions he could want or need. He's like the man in W. H. Auden's poem "The Unknown Citizen." That man owned a car and a Frigidaire, but—

Was he free? Was he happy?
The question is absurd: Had anything been wrong,
we should certainly have heard.

I'm sad to say that the man in this phase is likely, more or less symbolically, to rape and ravage the earth—and other people— to acquire what his mother could not give him as a child. This same man appears as a part of many men's psyches—who relishes playing video games that depict killing and torture, and who says things like "They ought to nuke 'em" when discussing anyone who displeases him.

Each of us who lost his mother early in life plays out some version of these responses to life. Each man left by a lover or a wife goes through the three stages of protest, despair, and detachment. Eventually he reaches the fourth and final stage: true separation, which often leads to divorce.

Frank exemplifies these stages. He couldn't believe that his wife had really left. He tried to get her back, became depressed, ate to numb his pain, and drank himself into oblivion. Finally he threw himself into his work, bought a new boat, and started dating his secretary, whom he married only two months after he signed the divorce papers.

Frank didn't fill the hole in his soul after his wife left. He medicated it, numbed it, and forgot about it. In other words, he did not use the experience to grow; he used it to "get"—in this case—another wife. He didn't expand his connection to his own emotions.

Exercise for Sons

If possible, men should find all of the information available about their births. This is not a confrontation; this is a gathering of information, so it's acceptable to go to your mother/ father, if possible, to ask about your birth and early infancy. If they're not available, perhaps you have aunts, uncles, or older siblings—anybody who can shed light on this time. Neighbors and old friends can also be very useful in gathering information that will help in dismantling the Mother-Son Dynamic.

Exercise for Mothers

Try to recall as much as you can about your son's birth. Did you like how it was done, or do you wish it could have been different?

Chapter 2

Patterns and Predictability

THE WIND LEFT . . . I WEPT. I SAID TO MY SOUL,
"WHAT HAVE YOU DONE WITH THE GARDEN
ENTRUSTED TO YOU?"

—*Antonio Machado*

Many patterns in the Mother-Son Dynamic are created
to maintain the illusion of control and to deflect what is going on
at the deepest level in the individual. Our patterns keep us from
breaking this dynamic and finding out what true mothering is. To
break those patterns, we must ask ourselves: How and when were
they created? How did they become the tyrants who imprison us?

Not surprisingly, the patterns usually began when we were children. They represent our best creative responses to stressful, traumatic, and hurtful situations. Our patterns were the defenses that were effective in keeping Mother and Father or older siblings from invading our space and our souls; they were protection from whoever wanted to shape our sanity according to their standards. Either we were drawn to the pattern because we see it has more efficiency, or we choose the opposite because we see the inefficiency in whatever has been modeled.

The patterns we developed early on worked at that time. But often, just as we still cling to our patterns, our lovers cling to theirs. In relationships, we come to see each other's patterns emerge. When they do, everything about the pattern works right on schedule. I do this, she responds a certain way. When she does, I respond in my old familiar way, and so on. Patterns rob us of spontaneity. When patterns are operating, we experience a false or temporary sense of safety because we already know the outcome. But patterns deceive us; they're the illusion of control. "We cannot go back to dependence on techniques and attributes that have been earlier an essential help on our journey," wrote Jungian scholar Helen Luke.

EMOTIONAL INCEST

A few years ago I was in Clearwater, Florida, at a conference for Adult Children of Alcoholics. My mother, who lived only a few miles away, decided to attend the conference. A friend drove us all to the site. I had been on the road for several weeks in a row, lecturing and doing workshops, and was near exhaustion. I was talking about how tired I felt when all of a sudden my mother started massaging my shoulders. I wept gentle tears as I realized I had no memory of my mother ever comforting me this way before. Here I was, a grown man, unable to remember a time in my childhood when I did anything but rub her shoulders and soothe her brow. I kept hearing her words: "Come give me a neck rub. Bring me a wet rag to put on my head." The unspoken message was: "Dance for me, my darling. Mama needs you to be her little man."

At the end of a lecture I gave in Vancouver, a woman said, "I heard you talk about how to love appropriately and how to connect with your children. Sometimes I feel so lonely. My husband and I have been divorced for five years, and I just haven't been able to find anyone that I really am attracted to. When I'm feeling really lonely, I call my six-year-old son over and ask him to give me a hug and hold me. And he does, and I feel better, but should I be worried that I'm doing something really wrong and harmful to him?"

I replied that a six-year-old's body and soul are not equipped to meet the psychosexual needs of a mother who longs for adult companionship. Nor would it be appropriate for a son, of any age, to give such companionship to his mother. It is the mother's responsibility to create a network of supportive friends and family who can meet those needs. Her natural longing for touch should be met by people who are equipped to deal with the mutual outflow and inflow of energy that comes between two adults during closeness and intimacy. This will give her a full reservoir of energy, so that when her son needs a hug, she has plenty to give, rather than bringing her own neediness to him. Otherwise, her loneliness will pull at the boy's body, draining it, making it difficult for him later on to enter adult relationships based on an equal flow of giving and receiving. This awkward, unhealthy exchange of energy will teach him to find lovers who'll take from him the way his mother did. Or he will look to his children to fill his longing. He'll remain unsure about when to stay, when to leave, or whether he'll ever be able to live according to his internal rhythms of closeness and distance. It wasn't the answer the woman wanted, but she appeared to hear it just the same.

This kind of love is what Dr. Patricia Love describes as "emotional incest," because a child is not emotionally equipped to support an adult's emotional and psychological needs. This may contribute to or cause a man to look at a woman and see her body but not her soul. If he is driven from the breast at too early an age but is later called on to soothe his mother's body, then women become mere bodies. If the man projects his feminine soul onto women—mothers and mates—he will be unable to live in his own body and will seldom feel like he owns his soul. So the adult son stores in his body his feelings of resentment. He tries to snatch the woman's soul in myriad ways, tries to cram it into his body to complete himself. All the while somehow he knows it's not her soul he wants but his own that he has lost in an unspoken agreement with his mother.

Anaclitic depression is a kind of depression that borders on despair at a lack of nonsexual, nonerotic love, usually given from the mother (sometimes from the father). It is a little-known, even less discussed type of depression that both men and women can experience but is very likely present in men who were enmeshed with their mothers. This serious form of depression is caused by a child's receiving libidinous love and as an adult still yearning for it, even if he's never heard if it or had it diagnosed by a clinician. My therapist, Dr. James Maynard, for many years introduced the concept and the constraints this form of depression can create. This type of depression can come from the act and fact that the mother, for whatever reasons, tends to depend on her son, sometimes in an emotional/sexual manner rather than in a clean, clear and consistent, nonusurping way.

Consequently, the son becomes super dependent on his mother as the alpha and the omega of his existence. This is especially true if the boy's father is absent emotionally or physically or both. The mother turns to the son for comfort, and the son says, does, or tries to become whatever his mother seemingly needs him to be—because in his mind if he loses her like he lost his father, he would truly be abandoned and die. This son becomes the beginning and end to his mother, a dynamic that can go on for decades, creating a level of depression no one seems to talk about.

Let's look at some examples of emotional incest involving an adult son. Charles went out to dinner with his mother, and they ran into a couple of her friends. She introduced Charles, saying, "Isn't my son handsome? The only way that I could get a man this handsome to go out with me was to make one myself."

Ronald brought his twenty-year-old daughter to a workshop I was teaching in New York. He said, "She's my date; I take her everywhere I want to go and leave her mother at home." In both these instances, the parents may have thought they were complimenting their children, making them feel special, rather than putting them into an inappropriate role. However, the covert communication to the daughter is "You're equally or more attractive to me than your mother is." This statement, which at first seems like an innocent compliment, is a heavy burden for any girl or young woman to carry.

Emotional incest appears when the mother tries to live vicariously through her son, and it is the unconscious act of draining the boy's energy to make her feel better, less tired, less lonely, and more fulfilled. It is characterized by mothers or fathers giving their sons or daughters age-inappropriate information; using them as surrogate counselors or confidants to talk about a parent or grandparent or sibling and looking to them to figure out what to do; talking about a child's body, genitalia, or commenting on his weight; or, as in the last two examples, having a son or daughter stand in where an adult partner would. Emotional incest is the fertile ground that most codependency stems from, and it is usually emotional incest that leads to sonning, mothering, rescuing and being rescued, and "when you do, I do" behavior.

Exercise for Mothers and Sons

Following are some common behaviors that can indicate at worst emotional incest and at best enmeshment between mothers and sons. See if any of them apply to you.

- The mother is still involved in helping the adult son coordinate or purchase his clothing.
- The mother always sides with the son if the son and his father are in a heated debate or argument.
- The mother gets highly energized by the son's presence and then feels depleted or despairing in his absence.
- The mother makes unsolicited comments, suggestions, and criticisms about the son's wife, girlfriend, or partner.

SONNING IS ONE OF THE STRONGEST PATTERNS

Sonning is a term Dr. Joseph Cruse taught me to describe how men perform the role of a son without even realizing it; a role that keeps men thinking and acting like little boys. When men act like sons, their parents act in kind, and men get pissed off, frustrated, and end up feeling small. Perhaps, if men are still sonning with their parents as adults, they're sure to be doing the same with their wives or lovers, leading to dysfunction that can rival that of their childhoods.

A key to breaking the negative Mother-Son Dynamic is to stop being a son to anyone. Forty-year-old Robert told the men gathered around him how he spoke one night on the phone to his mother. It was clear that he was sonning up a storm, and his mother was mothering in the only way she ever knew how. "Now, honey, tell me everything. Are you having sex with your wife?" Robert replied, "Yes, ma'am." But this pattern was so natural to Robert that he did not see it as unusual or even destructive until it was pointed out to him.

A man letting his mother, wife, girlfriend, or lover treat him and talk to him like he is a boy will have serious ramifications. If he is her boy and she is his mom, one of those ramifications could be, as I have often seen, that he takes on a mistress—sometimes it is a woman, sometimes it is work, golf, making money, or pornography—because he can't make love to a mother.

The pattern of mothering and sonning carried into adulthood is detrimental for these reasons:

- It shows the mother in a superior role and the son in an inferior role. This inequality will often breed anger and resentment.

- It undermines the son's self-confidence and self-esteem to think that "Mom knows best."

- It undermines the son's authority over his children. (An example of this occurred when I would go with my mother to visit her mother, and her mother treated both Mom and me like her children.)

- The mother keeps perpetuating a role that is long past overdue to have stopped.

- It shows a lack of respect to the adult son.

Exercise for Sons

When I began the process of dismantling my Mother-Son Dynamic, I had to go back to go forward. One indicator that this dynamic is in play is interacting with our mothers in certain ways we did as children. Examine the way you were treated as a child and how many of those behaviors still remain in your adult life. A man must know/feel how long and how much he is still playing the role assigned to him in childhood.

Are you still acting, talking, and behaving like a son around your parents, bosses, partners, or spouse? Write down the ways you act that you identify as sonning.

Making some lists will help you discover if you may still be falling into childhood patterns and behaviors when you are with your mother. First, make a list of the cute, pet, fun nicknames your mother called you or still calls you; for example, sonny, my baby, Junior, my special one. Does your mother still refer to you as the baby or the oldest boy of the family?

Now make a list of the pet nicknames or childish names with which you still refer to your mother; for example, mommy, honey, sweetie.

Make a list of ways she treats you like a sonny or "my baby" and write down how those actions make you feel. Next, write down what it would feel like to remove or abolish these more infantile ways of addressing each other. Think about how you can do this.

Finally, look at the roles you still play upon returning home or going to family events. Describe your actions and behaviors at these family events that you would never do in your own home. Do you eat food you normally wouldn't at home? Do you drink more than you would at home? Do you go to bed earlier or later than you would at home? Would you let anyone call you Junior except possibly your mother and your father?

Exercise for Mothers

Make a list of the pet names you still call your grown son. Do you put him into a role (hero, mediator, peacemaker, handsome one, smart one, good one, bad one, rebel, savior) when he is visiting you?

ADULT SONS SEARCHING FOR MOTHERING IN OTHER WOMEN

The man who hasn't got enough energy drags himself out into the world, trying to find a lover, partner, or wife who will compensate for what was lacking in his childhood, or he will do whatever it takes to make himself forget what he didn't get—work, drink, drug, accumulate. He is almost always drawn to lovers who will on the surface appear to be nurturing and life-giving, offering him what his mother could not. Unfortunately for the man and his partner, even if she is able to actually give some of what he needs, he will not be able to let her get close enough to do so. Thus the struggle begins. He wants what he doesn't get but won't take; she tries to give and finally gives up, and both feel misunderstood and frustrated. Unfortunately, as the psychologist W. R. D. Fairbairn says, "Frustration is always experienced as rejection."

Sam is a good example of what so often happens. He is a pharmacist, an intellectual man who lives most of his life in his head. Whom did he marry? Amber, who hugs, touches, and strokes her world, and likes to cuddle kittens, children, and Sam. Sam was attracted to Amber because she was the opposite of the mother he grew up with. But now, after eighteen years of marriage, Sam wants Amber to talk to him more and listen to him more. He wants her to be more like the mother he grew up with, who at least talked to him, although she didn't listen. Amber, who is not and never was an intellectual, is understandably confused. And so the marriage begins to break down.

Or consider Doug and Bridgette. Doug's mother was highly intelligent, and from the time he was four or five years old, she talked to him like an adult. But his mother just didn't have the time or disposition to touch, hold, and physically nurture him. He grew up possessing a sharp mind, but his body was dulled by too much work, food, and alcohol, and not enough touch. Doug, a thinker/talker, was attracted to Bridgette, who was not only beautiful but had a sharp mind. She graduated second in her class at Berkeley and became a respected economist. They married, and when I met Doug in a two-day intensive therapy session, she was at the peak of her career, and he was at the depth of despair because he still needed that affection he didn't get as a child. Not long ago Doug told his men's group of the affair he was having with Paula, who loves to cuddle and hug, who wraps him up the moment he walks through the door.

Now Doug is faced with a dilemma. If he stays with his wife, he can continue to try to change her into the mom he never had. Or he can stay with Paula, and after a few months start trying to change her when he wants to have an intellectual conversation and sees she isn't perfect. There's a third alternative: he can go into his wound and do the necessary work to heal his wound.

Sam and Doug want what they didn't get from their mothers, and yet because they've never truly felt the pain that roams through their bodies and their relationships over this lack, they don't stop expecting others to give it to them. At some point in the grieving process, each man has to accept that the one and only time that someone was supposed to give him everything—his childhood—is gone forever.

Sam and Doug can keep trying to change and control their wives, or they can accept them as they are. If the latter, they must then decide whether what their wives are is enough. If so, each couple will presumably stay together. If not, everyone involved can look for a new partner. Accepting your partner means accepting that you have wounds and needs that perhaps your partner cannot meet. As an adult, you must find safe, sane, healthy ways to get those needs met by friends, family, and a support system. This is not an easy task for anyone. As one person said to me at a workshop, "It sounds to me that you're saying it takes a whole community to have a relationship." Right. If we create a supportive community, there wouldn't be nearly as many separations, break-ups, and divorces. The thinker/talker type may be afraid to watch his partner create a system that provides them both with hugs and physical nurturing. The feeler/toucher type may feel shut out when the thinker/talker goes in search of someone to talk to. But in each case, the partnership should benefit as long as boundaries are made and held. Such issues may have to be treated in therapy, counseling, or a support group of some kind.

WOMEN WHO MOTHER
ADULT MEN

Sometimes women mother adult men, even if they are not their sons. A wife, lover, or partner who treats her partner like a child can exacerbate the situation if he is caught in the Mother-Son Dynamic with his mother. A man playing the role of son in his partnership will be more likely to continue to play out this pattern with his mother.

I was at Whole Foods one day having lunch, and all the tables were occupied. A frenzied-looking woman was searching for a seat. I said, "You are welcome to sit here."

"Oh you are so nice! I'm so exhausted, and I'm so glad I don't have to stand." She plopped into the chair opposite me. "You can't believe the kind of day I had."

I walked right into the next question, because I was almost sure I knew what was coming. "Kids, right?"

"You're right, four of them!" she said.

I raised my eyebrows. "Four!"

She smiled. "Well, three kids and my husband!"

I signaled the waiter. "Check, please!"

She told me everything in those words: "Four; well, three and my husband." That man, whoever he is, must see and feel some anger and resentment toward her. If you are a mother who suspects you may be enmeshed with your son, or a woman who may want to find out if you are compounding your partner's Mother-Son Dynamic, try the following exercise.

Exercise for Mothers and Partners

Read the following list and see how many apply to you. What part do you play in this behavior? Sons can also benefit from looking at this and determining what applies to their mothers. These are some things women do to mother adult men, whether they are sons or husbands, partners, or lovers:

- Do you find yourself doing "mothering" kinds of things for your husband, partner, or grown son that he should be doing for himself, which you rationalize would be easier, more efficient, or correctly done if you do it for him? Some examples are picking out his clothes to wear or telling him when he needs to shave and get a haircut.

- Do you often think of or express the feeling that your husband or lover is like another child of the family?

- Do you do small things for your husband/partner or adult son like you would do for a young son or daughter, such as reminding him where he put his car keys, helping him find his billfold, picking up after him, correcting his grammar in front of others or at home, and monitoring his table etiquette at social events?

- Do you do larger things for your partner or adult son, such as monitoring his physical health so he doesn't have to and doing all the housework, shopping, and cooking so he does none?

- Have you heard your husband or lover frequently say, "You're not my mother," or "Stop talking to me like I am your child"?

- Do you find yourself lying or stretching the truth, calling in sick for him when he is well but just hungover and afraid to do it himself?

- At social functions or when guests are over, do you tend to tell him where to sit, and perhaps even direct the conversations to show him in the best possible light?

- Did you see your mother lose herself or be absorbed or enmeshed with your father and his goals and dreams?

- Have you tended to put your personality, problems, or pains on hold so you can "take care of him"?

COMPASSION FATIGUE:
THE RESCUER AND THE RESCUED

If you are coming down through
the narrows of the river Kiang,
Please let me know beforehand,
And I will come out to meet you
As far as Cho-fu-Sa.

—Ezra Pound, *The River Merchant's Wife*

Another pattern that is all too often played out in the Mother-Son Dynamic is the role of those who rescue and those who need (or appear to need) rescuing. Until our healing work began in earnest, Grace and my mother fit the latter category and I fit the former. This is the main pattern that has worn me out and worn out many men I know. There is a depth of tiredness in me, and probably in all rescuers, that has been there since childhood. It is called *compassion fatigue.* You see this in doctors, nurses, and counselors. No vacation, no amount of sleep ever touches this kind of tiredness. The rescuer is always alert, always on call—and almost always resentful that he has to be this way. For years I carried inside me the deep, dark truths about what happened in our family. I feared the pain I would cause my mom were I to let these truths out of my body, my mouth, my soul. And so I did not reveal them until recently. The last few months I have told Grace and my mother things that until a year ago I'd have never dared let loose. For example, I told Grace that the reason I had stopped having women as friends was that I feared how she would feel. But I realize now that just because she may have unresolved jealousy is no reason I need to deprive myself of the nourishing company of women. I told her I would be loyal to our relationship but was no longer willing to protect her from whatever she was feeling.

Similarly, I told my mother some of the ways I remembered hurting my sister, even though I knew my sister did not care to listen to me and my confessions. At least now my mother knew; for years I feared it would devastate her, but to my surprise it didn't. I had carried this guilt and shame for years. Not only did Mom listen to me but she said she had suspected such things had happened and was just waiting until I felt ready to share this burden with her. My psychic load decreased immeasurably. My mother apologized for not having interceded, and she embraced me while I cried tears I'd been holding in for too long. We both felt lighter and closer. For years I thought my mother was the one who needed rescuing. Now in some ways I see how I needed to be pulled out of a deep depressive sea of responsibility I had been drowning in for way too long.

In contrast to rescuers, people who have to be rescued always need just a bit more than they have; they need more money, more sleep, more hugs, and more comforting than any one human can provide. They resent having been cursed with this legacy and even unconsciously resent those who oblige their neediness by rescuing them, because this prevents them from discovering the internal and external resources they need to rescue themselves. My mom looked to her children; Grace looked to her lovers; neither one was ever really rescued.

MEN WHO WAIT FOR RESCUE

Men who have been deeply wounded by their mothers will look for women who want to rescue them from their childhood heartbreaks, adolescent depression, and adult despair. This is the woman who has been referred to in other literature as having the Florence Nightingale syndrome. These women see men as broken-winged birds that need to be mothered and restored to health and well-being, more often than not at the woman's expense. The man lets himself be tended to more like a patient than a person, a child rather than an adult, and will gladly take—but ultimately resent— all this woman does for him. Finally, once she has brought him up to his "full potential," the man flies off and finds another woman who can heal parts of him that the last one could not. So the cycle continues until he can see that he's not a wounded animal and finds a woman who does not try to nurse or mother him.

Exercise for Sons, Mothers, and Partners

The pattern of rescuer and rescued is common in the Mother-Son Dynamic. Do you recognize yourself in any of the following behaviors and traits that rescuers and those rescued tend to display?

Rescuers

- are often tired and exhausted because they're trying to manage their own lives and rescue someone else's life;

- create a false sense that they are superior to the people they are rescuing;

- think they're smarter, more capable, more conscious, and better equipped to handle problems than the rescued (which often breeds resentment in the rescued);
- tend to constantly give advice and suggestions and criticisms that undermine the rescued person's self-esteem;
- often make promises they can't keep, overextend themselves financially, and more often than not cannot say no.

People who wait to be rescued

- look for external solutions to their problems;
- have a tendency to put the rescuer on a pedestal, creating an unequal relationship;
- tend to have low self-esteem and self-worth and feel like failures;
- are often resentful and angry at the person who tries to help them. (Psychiatrist Harry Stack Sullivan famously quoted, "He was so angry at me you would have thought I had tried to help him.")

For both rescuers and rescued, answer the following questions:

- Did your mother look to you to rescue her?
- What behaviors as rescuer do you feel obligated to perform?
- Have you re-created these behaviors with a current or past partner? Have you found new and different ways to rescue your partner?

- Is this a role you learned to play and continue to play, even though it is not necessary or healthy in your current relationship or partnership?

THE PATTERN OF "WHEN YOU DO, I DO"

*Pray for a tough instructor to hear
and act and stay within you.*

—Rumi

The decision to deepen relationships with ourselves and others increases our desire to take more responsibility for our lives and our relationships. When we separate from our parents and truly become individuals, we discover from that point on we are totally responsible for who we are, what we do, and what we become. Often, people remain entrenched in an unhealthy Mother-Son Dynamic simply because we don't realize that we do not have to let another person's behavior dictate our own. Understanding the pattern of "when you do, I do" helps us examine if we are participating in our relationships as separate, individual selves, or if we are unconsciously slipping into behaviors as a reaction to our partners' or parents' actions.

For decades, psychologists have been telling us that our goal as human beings is to become "authentic," "individuated," "whole," "self-actualized," and "autonomous." Before that can happen we must discover how we became a "piece" in the first place and why we "fall to pieces" when a loved one leaves us. We must also learn how the roles we played to please our parents were developed in large measure to help them forget that they themselves were not whole.

If in childhood we learn to pull away from our parents at the right time and to the right degree, we would feel, see, and know that we were separate from our mothers. And we would be able to carry her image and love with us wherever we go. However, if we do not separate in a healthy manner, we go away feeling alone and unable to appropriately attach ourselves to those who love us and whom we love. Instead, we are attracted to commitment-phobic people and want them to commit to us, or we are drawn to emotionally unavailable people and pray they will become emotionally available.

Wholeness arises when a child is able to see himself as a separate, autonomous human being, able to come and go, unite and disconnect as needed. But usually as children we cannot tell where we leave off and our mothers begin. As children, then, we need to be supported in the separation process that, ideally, would lead to the vital discovery "I'm me and you're you." If this doesn't happen, we grow into adults with the erroneous belief that what we do or don't do, what we become or don't become affects not only the quality of our own lives but also the lives of our parents.

As a result we often see a form of behavior I call the "when you do, I do" rationalization. This defense mechanism allows many children and, later, men and women, to shrug off responsibility for their behaviors, no matter how damaging they may be.

For example, Maya, age four, goes to her mother seeking attention and perhaps a hug. For whatever reason, Mama is unable to give Maya what she needs just then. So Maya goes into her bedroom, gets out her crayons, and scribbles all over her bedroom wall. Mama comes in, sees the mess, picks up her daughter, and spanks her bottom. For the next few hours, Maya does not want to be near her mother, nor does she answer when the mother calls.

Let's deconstruct this pattern to see how the concept "when you do, I do" applies. Maya has a right to expect a certain amount of attention from her mother. When she doesn't get it, she draws her disappointment on the bedroom wall. She wouldn't have done what she did if her mother had not done what she did: reject her and fail to fulfill her needs. Because of her own dysfunctional childhood, Maya's mother was not able to separate from her mother, so now she is unable to separate from her daughter's behavior and actions. This mother tells herself that if Maya had not done what she did, she wouldn't have had to spank her. Thus, the mother makes her daughter responsible for her adult behavior.

I can't tell you how many men and women have told me in my workshops that, sure, they were whipped or beaten as children, but they must surely have done something to deserve it. Starting as young as two or three, they were taught to believe that they were responsible for their parents' reactionary behavior. But children must not be held responsible for a parent's behavior. They are not to blame if their parents beat them or get drunk or act in abusive ways.

Here's an example of how the "when you do, I do" pattern arises in an adult relationship. For some time now, Todd and his wife, Cassandra, have not been getting along. Their relationship is tense at best, abusive at worst. Todd believes that Cassandra is withholding sex from him as a form of punishment, a way to get back at him and get him to act the way she wants. So he begins an affair with Kathy. As Todd put it to me during a workshop, "I wouldn't be sleeping around if Cassandra wasn't so damn cold and controlling." In other words, he's saying, "I'm not responsible for my decision or my actions—Cassandra is." He believes that if Cassandra acted differently, he would, too. He and his wife were so enmeshed that they were unable to separate from each other enough to take responsibility for their behavior as individuals.

The term *enmeshment* is often used to describe two people who want to be together all the time, who lose their sense of themselves as individuals because they love each other so much. This sounds loving, but there is a shadow side. Todd and Cassandra are enmeshed as well; that kind of enmeshment is more hidden and is therefore more threatening to a relationship.

At some point in Todd's journey, he needs to discover that he never fully separated from his mother during infancy, childhood, adolescence, or young adulthood, and he still has to do it. If not, he'll be following the path of many other men who in a misguided effort to form a separate identity from their mothers in midlife decide that the way to achieve that goal is to leave their wives or lovers. When they find another partner, the need to separate will still be there.

At some point in their lives, and I believe this almost always happens in the middle years, men and women must take time to discover, at a gut level, how they learned to feel responsible for their parents' behavior, thoughts, and feelings. When he undertakes this work, a man like Todd, faced with the possibility of an extramarital affair, will make his choice based not on what his wife is or isn't doing, but on who he is: what he feels, thinks, and holds to be right or wrong for him. If such a thing as a moral imperative exists, I believe it is that we must become totally responsible for our own actions. At the same time, the other person with whom we are in relation must take total responsibility for his or her behavior. Here is one way to put the equation: the reason I don't steal is not because you don't steal but because I believe it's wrong. It doesn't matter to me whether you steal or not. Even if you did steal from me, I wouldn't. I don't steal from you no matter what you do or don't do, because as an individual, I don't steal. This way of thinking discredits the strategy "when you do, I do" and offers a healthier way of thinking: "Just because you do, doesn't mean I have to."

Starting in the late 1950s and early 1960s, the idea emerged that a relationship issue or problem is 50/50. That was a good beginning, but as Pia Mellody has taught, each adult should take 100 percent because nearly everything I'm hurt or upset about is more about me and my history than it is about you and me together. Imagine a relationship that consists of two people who each take 100 percent, which equals 200 percent, twice as much as taking 50/50.

I'm reminded of a woman I talked to recently on the phone. Brenda said that the other day she was feeling good, but then her husband came home in a horrible mood and "the rest of the evening was ruined." In other words, she held him responsible for the evening, her mood shift, and her behavior. This kind of enmeshment occurs all the time. When it does, things always end badly, with someone blaming someone else. One plays the child, one the parent, and the present moment slips into the past, causing pain that has been caused over and over again.

Had Brenda somehow been able to breathe, burst through, and take total responsibility for her mood, her feelings, and her evening, what might have happened? What would she have felt like, what depth of peace would have been possible for her? And, for that matter, her husband?

Exercise for Sons, Mothers, and Partners

By answering the following questions, you can learn if you are trying to make others responsible for your actions. Sometimes it is not readily apparent, particularly if this is a pattern you have witnessed and practiced your whole life. I'll address the process and value of taking responsibility for yourself in just a bit.

- Make a list of friends, family, bosses, and employees whom you feel negatively toward. How is it that you have blamed them and thus justify the inappropriate reactions to them?

- How have you retaliated because of something they said or did?

- Now write down who blames you for any number of things they say you caused and to justify their behaviors and words.

- Go back and take a look at your childhood. Did you feel that you were in some way responsible for a parent mistreating you?

- Were you ever blamed for things that you did not directly cause, like Maya?

THE ENERGY CRISIS CAUSED BY THE MOTHER-SON DYNAMIC

Energy is eternal delight.

—William Blake

The quest for the Grail on which Parsifal—and we—must embark is also a quest to rediscover the energy we were born with. A key characteristic of the Mother-Son Dynamic is the huge amount of energy it steals from sons, their mothers, and their partners. Unfortunately, by the time many of us reach midlife, we are tired of the quest, ready to give up the search for our true selves because we lack energy. I remember how my father looked when he was fortyish, like he'd simply run out of steam. His eyes were emptier than his bank account, and his heart was a closed door to all who came knocking. He was not energized enough to be the man in Rilke's poem:

Sometime a man stands up during supper
and walks outdoors, and keeps walking because of
a church that stands somewhere in the East.

My dad and I and too many men are like the second man in the poem:

And another man, who remains inside his own house
dies there, inside the dishes and in the glasses.

I've felt like I've been in an energy crisis for most of my life. While I have a lot of energy now, when I was a child I didn't because I had to spend it being around my family, especially my mother. I talk about this a little bit in *Flying Boy II: The Journey Continues*, where I made the point that my family created what I call "energy straws." We kept these straws within reach; if we ever felt we needed some energy, we'd stick them into each other and suck away. The straw my mother attached to me made me feel like I didn't have enough energy to run my life. To survive my later years, I built my own "sucking device" to inject into my lovers from time to time. More often I was in relationships with people who, like my mother, needed my energy. For decades I readily gave it to them until I became depleted and disgusted. The only cure then was to create distance between us—break off, fly away (see *The Flying Boy: Healing the Wounded Man*).

Because my mom had brought so many of her psychic, emotional, and physical needs to me instead of sharing them with other adults who were more equipped to handle them, I was simultaneously drawn to people who depended on me alone to meet too many of their needs and, later, repelled by their neediness. Dr. Shafica Karagulla observes, "Any individual who remains in the vicinity of the sapper for long begins to feel desperately exhausted for no reason he can understand. This baffles and bewilders him." I was always afraid of my own neediness, so I would try to appear as if I didn't really need anyone too much or too often. I believed this is what being a man and a hero was all about: Heroes and men give their energy to others, acting as if they have little or no needs themselves, but never letting anyone get too close for fear the other person will suck them dry. Heroes believe their purpose in life is to take care of others and that no one but themselves can be trusted to take care of them.

CODEPENDENCY'S ROLE
IN THE MOTHER-SON DYNAMIC

One of the first steps in breaking the Mother-Son Dynamic is to discover or rediscover how codependency still saps your vital energy. Whether you are a man or woman reading this, at some point in our lives we all must be taught, in the words of T.S. Eliot, to "Teach us to care and not to care, Teach us to be still."

Codependency has become a familiar term these days. You hear it mentioned often in sitcoms. But the concept is still very misunderstood and remains one of the leading causes of divorce, misunderstandings, pain, and relationship problems at home and work. There is almost no relationship we have where some codependency is not present, and in the Mother-Son Dynamic we are dismantling, codependency can be the way mothers and sons have related for decades.

As I've mentioned, codependency is an unfair, uneven exchange of energy. The codependent son gives and gives and gets little, if anything, in return. The codependent enters a room feeling good, happy, and full of energy, only to see someone sad, tired, and lonely, and then feels compelled to "fix." The classic codependent then leaves feeling sad, tired, and lonely but satisfied that the other person feels much better than before they spoke together. Codependency is the way people numb their feelings. Okay, perhaps you're not addicted to alcohol, drugs, work, rage, sex, or gambling. But codependency will numb a person's feelings of sadness, anger, hurt, fear, or loneliness as well as any traditional medications—or addictions—can. By focusing on someone else's feelings, you don't have to deal with your own. There's the old joke that when a codependent person dies, they see everyone else's life flash before their eyes but not their own.

This energy imbalance created a barrier between me and Grace. When she may have needed just a little of my energy, I'd think she needed a lot. And when she actually did need a lot, she looked more and more like my mother waiting to drain me dry. And so I'd create distance by leaving or by starting an argument. Most often I won, and when I did, energy would rush back into my body—at least temporarily—and make me feel full and whole. Grace, though, would be left drained and confused. This is codependency, what I've previously defined as "an unfair, uneven exchange of energy" (*Flying Boy II*). I go on to say that the codependent person is "so afraid to tell you what they really think, feel, or need for fear of how it might make others feel, so they don't tell them." You can see how this applies to the young man mentioned earlier who didn't want his mother to know he "cursed." I believe this is what arguments, fights, even wars are: attempts by one side to deplete the other of its energy.

Codependency is in many ways the disease of selfishness. When you micromanage another person's life, you don't notice that your own life has become completely unmanageable. You end up looking like the healthy, more compassionate, intelligent, spiritual one—at least on the surface—and yet you can get just as addicted to this behavior as the heroin addict is to heroin. Codependents are forever relying on external sources to make and keep them happy. Remember Heart's Sorrow? If their babies are safe and nearby, they are happy. If they have enough money, they're happy; if they don't, they're unable to be calm and at peace. If their wives or husbands are doing well, then they feel they are doing well. If

Mama is happy or Daddy is happy, then everyone in the family is temporarily comfortable and secure. There is little or no ability in codependents to internally create peace of mind, serenity, self-esteem, and self-worth as they focus on others and, in the process, look damn good but are really burned out.

Codependency is an immersion in and preoccupation with everybody's business but our own. It is making sure everyone else's needs are taken care of while neglecting your own needs. Picture this scene at a holiday gathering. Mother is waiting hand and foot on everyone: "Does everyone have enough turkey?" "Who needs cranberry sauce?" "Let me get you some bread." She runs herself into the ground. Someone finally says, "Mother, sit down and eat. Everything is fine." Mom looks tired but is still eager to please. "I'll sit down after everyone is through." "I'll grab something while I'm cleaning up the table and in between washing dishes, dear." "You go ahead and enjoy yourself; I'll eat next year." It isn't that funny—but isn't it also a little too true?

The process of dismantling the Mother-Son Dynamic entails a great deal of new thinking, behaviors, and actions, which go against society's injunction to appear selfless. Yes, I know you have read Melody Beattie's bestseller *Codependent No More*, and you know many of your friends and family members who are flaming codependents. At the very least you have heard the word on some of your favorite sitcoms, and for sure you have read about it in magazines. One way to recognize negative patterns, such as the ones I've named—sonning and mothering, rescuer and rescued, and "when you do, I do"—is that they all indicate codependency and all involve an uneven exchange of energy.

Next, we'll take a look at some characteristics of codependency to determine whether or not it may be in play in your life. Later, in the next part of the book, we'll address some solutions to this.

Exercise for Sons

First, write down the things you have always wanted to say to your mother but have never felt able to. Have you refrained from telling her for any of the following reasons, which can indicate codependency?

- You were afraid it would hurt her feelings.
- "It would just kill her."
- No one talks to their mother the way you really want to talk to yours.
- It wouldn't do any good, so why bother?
- You've told her before, but it didn't change anything.

Exercise for Mothers

These are behaviors and phrases commonly used by mothers in codependent relationship with their grown sons. Do you often find yourself saying statements like these, or behaving in these ways?

- "I'll be heartbroken if you don't come to visit me."
- "You'll never know how hard it is to be a mother."
- You always put yourself last, both with your son and perhaps the whole family. You exhaust yourself doing so

and then frequently complain that no one ever puts you first.

- You remind your son of all you had to give up to be a mother.
- You think that your adult son "owes you" consideration, comfort, and concern in your old age, whether or not he can provide it.

RECOGNIZING RAGE AS PART OF THE MOTHER-SON DYNAMIC

The Buddha taught that "Holding on to anger is like grasping a hot coal with the intent of throwing it at someone else; you are the one who gets burned."

If a Mother-Son Dynamic has been in place for many years, or a whole lifetime, unexpressed anger can build up and become inappropriately expressed rage. I'll explain the difference between anger and rage and show how rage is disguised as other behaviors. As soon as we know to look for them, though, it's clear that they stem from unexpressed anger. The great cowboy writer Louis L'Amour said, "For each rage leaves him less than he had been before—it takes something from him."

Unfortunately, many of us—myself included—use certain words interchangeably, as if they mean the same thing. Many say *self-pity* when they mean *grief*. Others confuse *sympathy* and *empathy*. But the words *anger* and *rage* are constantly spoken in the same sentence by therapists, counselors, and the general public, educated and noneducated alike. They do not mean the same thing. Anger is a feeling that comes and goes and doesn't do any damage to the body or the soul. It is an emotion that moves in, through, and out of the body and can usually be expressed quickly. Rage, on the other hand, is not—I repeat, is not—a feeling but an action or behavior that is used to temporarily numb our feelings and medicate our emotions. Rage is just as effective in numbing our feelings of sadness, fear, loneliness, and even anger, just as any drug, narcotic or stimulant, alcohol, food binging-and-purging, sex addiction, or workaholism can. Rage is legal, plentiful, and readily available. When I am shaming, blaming, or demeaning you, I am raging at you. I am not feeling anything. When I am demoralizing, criticizing, teaching (in a patronizing manner), judging, analyzing, or preaching at you, I am not telling you how I feel. I am not opening my inner emotional self to you. I am in my head (where many wounded sons retreat when scared or when they want to say something to someone), not feeling a thing but subconsciously wanting you to feel terrible about what you said or did, didn't say, or didn't do that scared me, hurt me, or made me sad or angry.

When I am interrogating you, intimidating you, distancing myself from you, or playing the "poor me," I am using behaviors and taking action to make my feelings go away temporarily, just as drinking alcohol or ingesting a drug will do. So when my clients or workshop participants tell me that their husbands, wives, or parents are very angry, what they really mean to say is that they are raging. For example, my ex-lover's mother was not an angry woman—she was a woman full of rage, she behaved and acted like a woman full of rage, and she made many sexist, racist, and gay-bashing statements. When a mother beats her children with her hairbrush, she is not angry, she is outraged. She is acting, behaving, and not feeling, because if she were truly feeling her feelings, she would also feel in her body that she must not hit her children.

Following are a number of ways to tell the difference between anger and rage:

- Rage takes a long time to express—hours, days, weeks, months, years, and lifetimes. Anger expressed appropriately takes moments or minutes at most.

- Rage is never resolved in a short conversation. Anger is often resolved in a sentence or two, maybe even three or four.

- Rage consists of paragraphs, pages, and volumes.

- There is no relief when rage is expressed. Anger expressed relaxes us and sometimes even the other person because they feel safer with us now that they know how we feel.

- Rage always equals distance, disaster, and, frequently, divorce. Appropriate anger equals closeness, order, and clearer communication.

- When men, women, or children rage, everyone feels tired and drained. When we express anger appropriately, we usually feel refreshed and rejuvenated.

- Rage tends to hurt everyone in the vicinity. Proportional anger tends to hurt no one.

Let me be a little repetitive here and say again: rage is an action or a behavior used to numb our feelings. Appropriately expressed anger is neither positive nor negative and generally hurts no one any more than expressing sadness or joy does.

FOUR STYLES OF RAGE

There are four predominant styles of rage. All four are frequently used, but some people gravitate more to one or two styles. Remember, when a man rages, he is temporarily looking and sounding strong, but at these moments he is really at his weakest.

The Interrogator

The Interrogator is the rager who has ways to make you talk. "What time did I tell you to be home?" "Who were you with?" "How many times have we had this conversation?" "How much did you have to drink?" "What is your excuse?" "How many times have I told you?" "When are you going to visit?" "Why don't you ever call?" The Interrogator employs a rapid series of questions to control, manipulate, shame, or judge, leaving everyone exhausted and willing to sign any confession just to get out of the cold cement room with a dim lightbulb and a one-way mirror.

The Intimidator

The Intimidator is the man or woman who rages by getting big and loud and filling up the room with a gigantic roar, which demeans and demoralizes those around him or her and makes others feel small and silent. The Intimidator curses loudly and throws objects off tables or desks. He or she often employs preaching, sarcasm, and put-downs. Sometimes Intimidators fill up the room with a silence that is deafening. Everyone around them is whispering and shushing everybody, hoping the Intimidator won't snap. Intimidators believe might makes right, and they're always going to have the last word.

The Poor Me

The Poor Me is just as full of rage as the Intimidator and the Interrogator but does not have enough energy to question or get large. Poor Me ragers feel like the victim in every situation and use complaining, justifying, and draining language to get their points across. The martyr mother (and sometimes father) will often employ this style. "Am I the only one who has to work around here? I clean up the house before going to work. I work all day long, fight the commute home, and when I get here the house is a mess again." "You'd think after working all day and putting up with all that I have to put up with, I could come home and relax, but noooo!"

The Distancer

The Distancer is the most prevalent style. This is the man who can't make a clean break with Mom so he moves to Alaska and thinks about going farther to Russia because "You can see it from Alaska," to quote a confused mother. The Distancer has one foot in and one foot out of every conflict, confrontation, and argument. He or she uses one of the worst four-letter words in relationships, one that communicates nothing: *Fine*. Cherie says she hears this word from her husband all the time before he walks out the door. The Distancer also uses the word *whatever* quite a bit. Both words basically say, "I'm out of here and I'm not going to tell you where I'm going or when I'll be back; you can do whatever you want and I'll say it's fine, but really it isn't fine at all."

HOW PEOPLE EXPRESS RAGE

One of the many passageways to intimacy is through the facilitation of appropriate anger work. Sadly, most men and many mothers, women, and children tend more often to rage than express anger appropriately.

There are many reasons for sons to be angry with their mothers, many of which we have just discussed. There are many more. If mothers or lovers or wives infantilize (treat like children) the men in their lives, the men will become angry and resentful and more often than not will hold this in until they are ready to explode. Many think they are expressing their anger when they really are not. Many people have been taught, especially since the sixties, that we are not supposed to "hold in" our feelings of anger and that we are to "confront," "encounter," or have someone "call us on our stuff." This was a movement in the right direction, but most people do not feel safe with any of these bold terms of expression. Infantilized sons will often seek revenge for this, even if they have to wait fifty years until their mothers are tired, aged and fragile. Then they will infantilize the elder mother, which not only terrifies the elder mother but often truly angers her.

The following are some things people do when they think they are expressing anger, but in reality what you are about to read are all forms of rage. I will lead you through a brief exercise after this, as well as explain exactly how these are all forms of rage, not anger.

Manipulating

The Mother-Son Dynamic is fraught with manipulation. A statement like "I want you to come over and fix the toilet for me" can be code for "Come see me; you never come see me." Manipulating people is by far one of the more common ways anger leaks out, usually unknowingly. When we are angry, we manipulate those around us, giving us a momentary sense of power—the opposite of feeling angry, which usually leaves us feeling powerless. An example is Jim, who was angry at his wife. He felt she did not appreciate the way he worked all the time to "keep her in the style which she had grown accustomed to as a child." So he would attend social functions by himself, even though both had been invited. He would convince her that she wouldn't enjoy the place or the people he associated with and that she would be much happier staying at home. Jim would then drink too much and flirt with every woman there.

Controlling

Control is the kissing cousin of manipulation. Angry sons and mothers are usually very controlling people. They try to control people, places, and things. They are like giant chess players moving the pawns around the board, mostly because they're angry and just do not know it. The insecure or dysfunctional mother can be a controller par excellence. Angry sons constantly try to create the illusion of control. Robert "gave" his wife an allowance each week as a way to keep her from spending their money on cocaine. He checked her odometer in her car each evening to see whether she used more than her allotted miles to go to the grocery store or pick up the children from school. When asked about this, he said he was just "helping" his wife not use. This was much like his mother's behavior when she would search his backpack and chest of drawers and read his journal, trying to catch him using drugs (which he never did).

Sabotaging

Rodney's mother abandoned him when he was ten years old. She ran off with the minister of her church, and he didn't hear from her again until he was twenty-eight years old. He was angry at her for leaving him with his alcoholic father, who was never emotionally there for him. In every relationship he got into, Rodney undermined his success and expressed his anger at women inappropriately, thereby sabotaging all hopes of having a healthy relationship. Just when a relationship was beginning to go deeper, he would withdraw from her emotionally, shut down, and then become involved with another woman. He was determined never to feel abandoned again.

Joking

Telling off-color, demeaning jokes is another form of anger leaking out of our overpressurized boilers. People who tell racist jokes or jokes about gay people are really just ticked off about something. Making jokes that degrade or disrespect women is often a way an angry son transposes his rage at his mother. One way people justify their verbal punches in "putting people down" is to throw out the outworn phrase "I'm just joking." Any time you have to add that phrase, it probably isn't a joke. Almost everyone has had a "friend" who puts them down. Bill's mother would put him down in public and then right after doing so would always add, "I'm just kidding. He knows I love him." Here in the South we have the ability to say anything nasty we want to about someone as long as we add "Bless his heart." "Sherry is the worst mother in the world—she doesn't bathe that child of hers, she drinks all day long, and ain't got the sense God gave a billy goat—bless her heart."

Shaming

Shaming folks is done so frequently we hardly even notice it, although we feel it engulfing our bodies like the toxic ooze it really is. When Jim's mother was disappointed with him, she would say, "You can't be my son. I must have gotten the wrong baby at the hospital. My son would never be so incompetent." "What do you know? You were raised in the sticks," Tom's wife said when she was angry. Shame is the hammer to beat us into submission, leaving mothers and sons feeling guilty and less than loved.

Blaming

Blaming is employed when folks are angry. They use statements like: "It's all your fault," "Look at what you've done *now*," "You wouldn't be in this mess now if you had listened to me, Your mother always knows what's best." "I know you better than you know yourself." Jessie said to her husband, George, as she was packing to leave him, "If you had only gone with me to counseling like I asked you to years ago, we wouldn't be getting a divorce *now*."

Demeaning

"Look at how your mother raised you. She spoiled you rotten," Robert said to his daughter. "Can't you tell time? When the big hand is on twelve and the little hand is on twelve, that's when we meet for lunch," I sarcastically said to a girlfriend decades ago while confronting her about constantly being late for engagements. In my house, demeaning phrases were served up regularly, especially at dinner.

Demoralizing

Demoralizing comes in different disguises. Jason's mother constantly said, "Your brother is the one with the brains in this family." In turn, Jason says to his wife, "I don't think you're ever going to understand *me* no matter how many times I explain it to you."

Criticizing

Criticism is so common that most of us think it's actually okay to receive or give it, whether it's asked for or not. Most folks know down deep that unsolicited criticism, even the kind that "is for your own good" or given "because I love you" stings like a thousand bees. Many mothers say they are just being helpful when saying things like, "Stop stooping and stand up straight," "smile," "fix your tie," "your hair needs cutting," and "get that hair out of your eyes."

Preaching

Preaching "the gospel according to you" is a familiar attempt to release anger, especially for Southerners who grew up always within earshot of a pulpit and an angry preacher pounding out his rage to those in the pews who believe he is talking straight to them while damning everyone to an eternity of fire and brimstone. Or how about the rigid twelve-step sponsor who says only "Get off the pity pot" or "Turn it over to your higher power?"

Judging

The judge is the angry person who thinks he or she is telling you how he or she feels but is really judging your actions, behaviors, motivations, character, and personality. In reality, when I judge you, I am telling you more about myself and nothing about you.

The really good judge also gets to play two other roles—jury and executioner. The judge gets to find her guilty beyond a shadow of a doubt and impose the sentence he sees fitting to the crime.

Analyzing

Randy would never tell any woman how he really felt, but he would always say, "No, I'm not angry. I'm just trying to figure you out. You know I haven't had a real feeling since the Reagan administration." Randy, like many intelligent, well-educated people, "thinks" he is saying what he feels, but he is mostly in his head, not in his heart.

Having an All-or-Nothing Attitude

"Either go and see a counselor, or we're through," Joseph said to his wife. He felt he knew the "only way for her to be helped" was to do what he said—the old "my way or the highway" form of rage. An extreme point of view can be a form of rage. "If you don't go into therapy, I'm leaving you." "If you leave now, I won't be here when you return."

Playing Word Games

"You call me critical, but I'm just concerned about your happiness." "I didn't say that exactly." "You're not listening. You say potato, I say po-tah-to."

We've all heard these things so often. We've seen these behaviors displayed in some way by our loved ones, and we've done them, too—so often that we've come to think this is just the way life is. All of these behaviors have little or nothing to do with the appropriate expression of anger.

Exercise for Sons, Mothers, and Partners

On a scale of 1 to 5 (1 = never; 5 = very often), circle the number to determine the extent to which you, your partner, or your mother tend to employ the following forms of anger:

Shaming	1	2	3	4	5
Blaming	1	2	3	4	5
Criticizing	1	2	3	4	5
Preaching	1	2	3	4	5
Judging	1	2	3	4	5
Analyzing	1	2	3	4	5
Sarcasm	1	2	3	4	5
Put-downs	1	2	3	4	5
Jokes at other's expense	1	2	3	4	5
Sabotaging	1	2	3	4	5
Controlling	1	2	3	4	5
Manipulating	1	2	3	4	5
Lying	1	2	3	4	5
Gossiping	1	2	3	4	5
One-upmanship	1	2	3	4	5

Now, look at the items where you circled 4s and 5s. These behaviors are one more indication that the Mother-Son Dynamic in your life needs to be addressed. In the next chapter, I'll offer ways for you to turn your inappropriately expressed rage into appropriately expressed anger.

Chapter 3

Taking Responsibility

THERE CAN BE NO TRUE FORGIVING OF ANOTHER
WITHOUT THIS TAKING UP OF RESPONSIBILITY FOR
THE DARKNESS AND UGLINESS THAT IS OURS.
—*Helen Luke*

Imagine you have felt every feeling—sadness, anger, hurt, disappointment, and even appreciation—for what your mother did and didn't give you as a child. Imagine you have raged into the night at the loss of the nurturing breast, making primitive noises that sound more animal than human; that you've grieved the gargantuan hurt that comes when you finally realize that your childhood is long gone. You've finally realized that most of the dysfunctional stuff you saw and heard as a child, and later imitated as an adult, has cost you your health, happiness, and very nearly your sanity. This is the path we are taking together with this book.

Feelings are learned and modeled by parental or authority fig-ures. As you read this and do the exercises, you are separating from those and achieving what Carl Jung called "individuation." Most men or women don't start this process until their mid-thirties or early forties, some start sooner, and others start much later. In other words, becoming your own individual and separate person takes a long time, especially if you don't get help from others who are on a similar journey or near completing that journey. Jung said, "The first forty years, we're just doing research."

I am now going to walk you through the process of taking total responsibility for your feelings, your disappointments, your hurts, your happiness, and your healing. No one is to blame. You change no one but yourself. No one is abusing you, and if you abuse some-one, you alone are responsible for stopping that abuse.

Assuming this level of responsibility is so difficult! The upside of dismantling the unhealthy Mother-Son Dynamic is that it centers us in our adult selves and in the present moment. Paradoxically, when we have grieved the past and the parenting we received or didn't receive, we are better able to enter the present and stay there, just the way we often did as children.

As much as anyone in the field, the writer Pia Mellody has con-tributed to our understanding of codependency and love addic-tion. In her book *Facing Love Addiction*, she makes it clear that it is a person's responsibility to keep him- or herself in an adult state as much as possible. It is not our partners' role to bring us out of our child state when we regress, as many of us do when our buttons are pushed, when we're under stress or are fatigued, or when we're abusing alcohol, drugs, or sex. That's our job. If Tom can't get out from under the covers and face another midlife morning, it's not Margaret's job to pull him out of bed. And if Margaret is afraid that Tom is going to get out of bed only to go have an affair with Tina, it's not Tom's job to soothe her fears. (It is Tom's job, however, not to have the affair.)

I can perhaps best illustrate this point by sharing with you something that happened to me. My usual morning routine is to enjoy a cup of hot coffee alone and then take a short walk before joining Grace for breakfast. This particular morning, though, I awoke from a series of rather disturbing dreams. As soon as I sat down with my coffee to think about my dreams, I realized I felt like a scared six-year-old who'd just awakened from a nightmare and didn't want to be alone. I immediately got up and walked downstairs to Grace's study. I wanted and needed to be with her at that moment. As soon as I walked in, she could see that I wasn't my usual adult self. A tear ran down my cheek. "I had some terrible dreams this morning, and I'm real sad," I said. "Are you willing to hold me for a few minutes?" She stopped what she was doing, got down on the floor, leaned against the wall, and opened up to me like a flower. I sat on the floor and allowed myself to lean against her and be held.

Although inside I felt like a six-year-old boy lying against an adult woman's body, I was in fact a midlife man nurturing the six-year-old in himself by asking for what the boy needed and trying to get it for him. Some days you just can't hug yourself or hold yourself; you need another pair of loving arms.

In the past when I felt this way, I might have stayed upstairs in isolation and toughed it out, or if some woman did open up to me like a flower, I would usually (to quote a line from poet Ethridge Knight) "fall on her like a stone, fall on her like a stone." Or I might have done what I did for years: manipulate my partner into mothering me. I might have said, for example: "Let's you and I go upstairs. You don't have to work this morning. Let's get back in bed and make love." (Translation: "Let's have sex so I can numb the pain of my bad dreams away.") If I had handled my fears that way, I would have been a six-year-old boy crawling into bed with Mama, and we both would have felt diminished. If I had allowed that to happen, then the boy who was scared by dark dreams would have gotten nothing; Grace would have gotten a son instead of the man she wanted to hold—a man who was holding and nurturing the frightened little boy inside him. In other words, when Grace folded her arms around me, I was receiving nonlibidinous, nonsexual love, with no need for reciprocal return and no need to feel depressed by the bad dreams.

In personal growth, then, the movement is from what Jung called the superior function (that which we do best in life) toward the inferior function (that which we do less well). Midlife brings most of us face-to-face with our inferior function. The thinker/talker, for example, must explore feeling and touching; sometimes she is afraid to do so, but deep down she knows she must begin to practice this way of being if she is ever to feel more whole. In contrast, the feeler/toucher knows he must develop the capacity to talk, to be taught, and to listen to his intellect—functions that may have been rejected, made fun of, shamed, or despised when he was a child. The feeler/toucher then discovers that he is much smarter and more capable of verbal communication than he ever realized.

When the more developed side of ourselves searches for and embraces the less developed side, we become more truly ourselves, because we no longer let one side rule us while allowing the other side to be provided for by our lovers. At that point we are ready to serve instead of fix, heal instead of hurt. As we learn to embrace and, yes, even love our darker sides, we become less dependent on our lovers and less needy for something we cannot have. In an ideal world, our mothers would have loved all sides of us. As we heal the wounds made because our mothers couldn't love us that way, we will be less likely to turn our lovers into mothers or brand them as witches when they can't love us the way we desire.

When I lecture on mothers and sons, more than a few folks say to me: "It sounds like you're saying you should never act like a boy or girl with your partner, so that they won't be inclined to mother you." And then they add, "That's impossible."

To which I reply: "You're right."

Somehow, I began to allow myself to experience (instead of ignore) my own needs and not to shame other people, including Grace, when they sought to get their needs met. As I delved deeper into my fear of prematurely running out of energy while in relationship to my partner or my work, I started seeing that I had a lot more energy than I thought I had. I could now protect my own supply of energy—something I could never do as a kid. This is called "setting boundaries," which no one in my family saw or modeled. The next step, I realized, was to learn how to receive energy gracefully.

These days, because I acknowledge my neediness and my fear of not having enough energy, I don't need as often as before to grab my "energy straws" and stick them into people—or other quick but empty sources of energy, such as money, sugar, TV, work, or perfection. Consequently, I'm feeling more energetic than ever. I now use only a third of the energy to give my lectures and workshops that I used to. And I need only a third of the energy it used to take to be in relationship with Grace. Finally, I'm beginning to feel there's enough energy to go around. Like other adult children from dysfunctional families, I have been constantly fearful that there's a limited amount of everything in the world, including energy. In many ways this scarcity principle rules our lives. In layman's terms, there is never going to be enough by the time "IT" (whatever it is) gets around to me. As I drop down into this ancient fear and feel the anger and grief of having had my energy stolen, I give up the role of hero that demands I must forever sacrifice my energy in the name of saving people, and in so doing I become just a little bit more human.

Humans share that weight with others, and when they do, everyone is less tired and drained. Those who have learned to drop the roles of rescuer, fixer, caretaker, victim, martyr, or hero let the world and everything in it nourish them. As I said in my book *The Anger Solution*, "Where there are roles there is also some amount of rage," because everyone wants to be seen and heard outside the roles in which they have been placed. Some have discovered that the Grail, the great cornucopia of life, has plenty for everyone, that we have an incredible ability to give back to the world and to the people in it. Fewer arguments occur.

In the next section, we'll begin with solutions that are helpful for everyone, though directed toward sons. Then we'll address mothers and wives/partners more specifically.

INFANTILE NEEDS, ADULT NEEDS, AND GHOST LOVERS

*The child who finds out, all too abruptly
and too soon, that he cannot count on his mother's
strength to be there for him . . . feels he
has only himself to count on.*
—Marjorie White and Marcella Weiner

Adulthood means taking responsibility not only for needs—food, shelter, and clothing—but also the desires of the soul. If we're still looking for someone to take care of these decades-old needs for us, if we're still overly angry or anxious that it's not happening, our relationships will show it—usually by dissolving right before our eyes.

There comes a moment in life, usually around the midpoint, when we know deep in our hearts that the last vestiges of the "not good enough" mother have to be removed from our bodies, our brains, and our present relationships. This awareness arises slowly, so that little by little the needs we thought we had are replaced by an understanding of our real needs.

During the early stages of any healing process, many of us feel we have more needs than anyone will ever be able to fill satisfactorily. This is because we have unconsciously confused our genuine adult needs with our unfulfilled infantile needs.

By definition, childhood is when a person is supposed to be needy, dependent on adults to meet all needs from physical shelter and nourishment to emotional, psychological, and educational nourishment. All children are needy, and never before in the history of humankind have so few people been charged with meeting the neediness that all children necessarily have. It's true that it takes a village to raise a child, and yet today so many are being raised in single-parent households where that single parent is working at least one full-time job. So from the get-go, a little boy or little girl is labeled as being too needy and they may carry that label the rest of their lives.

In infancy, we require another person to soothe us. In adulthood, we must learn to soothe ourselves or ask for the appropriate person to soothe us. An infantile need is to have an adult mirror his or her radiance, beauty, and reflect that he or she is wanted. An adult needs mirroring by another adult, but an adult won't die or be stunted if they don't get it. Adults who are in need of mirroring might create a severely dysfunctional relationship with their children, wanting their children to mirror back to them what they didn't get in childhood or are still not getting in adulthood. So let's be clear: an adult's needs are to be met by fellow adults and not by their children.

Children are supposed to see themselves in their mother's and father's eyes. They are supposed to see in their parents' faces the delight the parents have for the children being in their lives, a look that says, "I see you, I respect you, I'm happy you're here." A child is supposed to look in the mother's eyes and see the glory of that child's radiance reflected back into the child's eyes.

When people fall in love, the loved one provides a similar mother-mirroring. This is one reason new lovers in many ways act childish or childlike; the body remembers the comfortable feelings reminiscent of early childhood. However, lovers are not able to sustain that mirroring or radiance. If your parents didn't or couldn't provide that, you'll look in your lover's eyes and either still not see that reflection or mirroring, or when it stops (like it often does in relationships), you'll get angry and go looking for it again.

What I say next will surprise many of you because you've been told just the opposite, and, sadly, you've been made to believe just the opposite. The truth is, there's no such thing as an adult person being too needy. This is equivalent to saying that a man or woman is too sensitive or too emotional. No one who lives on the planet is *too* either of these. The problem is that in most people's lives, there are too few people to meet a person's needs. Therefore, they go to one or two people to meet all their needs, and to those one or two people they appear too needy.

Here's an example. Marion was the youngest of five siblings. Her mother had her hands full. Her father wasn't around most of the time to help with the children; when he was around, he mostly served as a disciplinarian. Needless to say, Marion didn't get much physical affection when she was growing up.

In her mid-twenties, Marion moved in with Phil. As in her other relationships, she found herself needing Phil to hold her and stroke her much more than he was able to do. She underwent counseling to help her decide whether or not to stay with a man who could not fill her very large need for touch. While it is clearly important for every human being to be touched, those of us who did not receive sufficient touching as children have a little child inside our adult selves who is constantly in search of a partner who will provide what we missed in infancy. Marion thought if she could just get Phil to touch her and hold her enough, they would have no insurmountable problems. After quite a few sessions, Marion began to see that her wound—not getting touched enough—had been caused by her parents' inability to give. She saw that no man, including Phil, was ever going to be able to hug all her hurt away. After she began her grieving process, Marion soon stopped expecting Phil to provide what her parents hadn't given her, and instead began letting Phil love her and give to her in the way that came naturally to him and was sufficient for her needs.

Here is an example from my own life. As a small child I began listening to my mother's problems and disappointments. When I grew up, I gravitated to anyone who had a sad story to tell. I even became a rather good listener; this is certainly where I got my basic training to become a psychotherapist. Later, in adult life, I found that I desperately needed people to listen to me. Of course, governed by my old patterns, I was drawn to those who wanted me to listen to them but couldn't listen to me nearly as well as I wanted since I was a child. I became a teacher, a writer, and a lecturer, looking for a roomful of people who would listen to my story for a change.

Yet when I talked to my lovers, even to Grace, I became furious because I felt I wasn't heard. I realized that as a child I had never really felt heard by my parents and that as an adult I was trying to get women to make up for that lack. In the process of working through this with Grace, she learned to listen a little better, and, more important, I learned to grieve that as a child I had listened much more than any five-year-old should have to do. With that knowledge came the understanding that my expectations were too high for any woman to meet.

So often we unconsciously form relationships for the purpose of getting our infantile needs met. But after the first blush of romance fades, we start saying things like, "She doesn't meet my needs," or "He's never going to give me what I need." With these words we begin embracing not each other but despair and depression. We pray desperately for some cataclysmic change in our partners that will cause them to suddenly face us, divine our needs (both infantile and adult), and say, "Yes, I'll be the parent you never had. Tell me all the needs you had as a child, and I'll work day and night to fill the longing left in your body from days and nights of neglect." But we never find this person, except in our dreams, fantasies, and romance novels. This "person" is what C.G. Jung calls the "Ghost

Lover." The Ghost Lover is a compilation of what a good mother should have provided in early infancy (such as mirroring, unconditional love, attention, security, affirmation, touch, tenderness, and strength, etc.) and what the media and romance novels, movies, and TV shows say lovers should be, combined with the unrecognized or inaccessible feminine element in a man's life.

An example is my friend Mary. She once said about her husband: "Luke just isn't ever going to get it. He's never going to change." What she meant was, "Luke is never going to be like me." So Mary withdrew into her job and her hobbies: reading romances and watching soap operas. These stories let her indulge in her fantasy of the perfect partner who always knows just how to enter the Mystery of his lover—the way Luke used to when they were dating. She was more in love with her Ghost Lover, the one in her imagination, her fantasy, than the flesh-and-blood man before her.

Men who are still not wrestling with this Mother-Son Dynamic are likewise far more in love with Ghost Lovers than those who have separated themselves from their mothers. The Ghost Lover is his own anima that he has not embraced, or possibly never thought about. The Ghost Lover is the perfect feminine balanced with the perfect masculine. She is Mother Mary and Lucrezia Borgia, the dominated and the dominatrix.

What we may find instead, if we're lucky, are men and women capable of loving us as best they can; on good days, they'll meet many of our adult needs, and on some occasions, usually without meaning to, they may even fulfill some of our childhood yearnings.

Eventually, if we stay together long enough and do enough grief and healing work, we find ourselves with men and women who are just as wounded or as healed as we are. The wounded child in us, left untreated and un-nurtured, will pick up the cry of another wounded child. Like water, we seek our own level. We discover that whomever we're with, both of us are in about the same shape. In other words, whomever we're with is where we are. The two of us then home in on each other's signals, falling in love with the differences we see in each other. Inevitably, we'll both begin trying to change each other, to force the other to supply what our mothers could not. The trouble is that this little scenario is not going to happen, no matter what a few self-help gurus may say. Our partners are not there to parent us or to heal our wounds. They are with us to discover their own wounds and to learn, through time and experience, how to heal them without doing too much damage to the relationship in the process. They are there to mirror our woundedness, but it is up to us to take responsibility to heal.

Exercise for Sons

- What are some common complaints you have about partners? Can you look back to your childhood and see how these complaints could stem from things your mother didn't provide for you?

- Whether or not you have a current wife, girlfriend, or partner, do you have a Ghost Lover? Write down all the qualities, characteristics, personality traits, attributes, and background of the Ghost Lover who comes into your dreams, daydreams, and fantasies. Does the Ghost Lover behave in ways that meet the needs your mother could not or did not provide?

Exercise for Partners

- Can you answer honestly and truthfully that you feel seen as the woman you are and that your lover or husband completely accepts the woman you are, or do you feel some covert or overt pressure to live up to some romantic ideal? Do you feel he sees you as he would like to see you or as you really are?

- Do you see in your lover or husband a constant desire to be mirrored and validated and affirmed beyond what most people are capable of doing over a prolonged period?

- If you and your partner have a daughter, do you see him attempting to use her as a surrogate mother by looking to her for adoration instead of the other way around? Or do you feel your husband or lover sees his adolescent daughter as a way to get his positive attributes mirrored back to him, perhaps in a way that you as his partner cannot or do not do?

PASSIVITY

For the ordinary man is passive. . . .
So far from endeavoring to influence the
future, he simply lies down and
lets things happen to him.

—George Orwell

Passivity can stop men and women from moving forward in recognizing and doing the work to break the unhealthy Mother-Son Dynamic in their lives. Passivity is caused by many things. Overdependency on the mother or being overly depended upon by her or others is a major contributor. Passivity has been one of the least studied, discussed, and explained aspects of human behavior. The fields of psychology, personal growth, and recovery have completely ignored it. Understanding passivity as it relates to the Mother-Son Dynamic is essential to enhancing emotional intelligence, creating healthy relationships, increasing self-esteem, and healing the bodies, minds, and spirits of individuals who are hurting or are hurting others. Passivity especially occurs in men who were smothered as little boys. This boy becomes, to use to a much outdated term, a "gigolo," a "kept man." As an adult, he demands that women do for him like his mother did. Passive men are half in and half out of relationships. The passive man or woman is more attached to not having what they think they want or desire, even though they protest loudly that this is not so. Passivity is the compulsion to pursue the opposite of what we say we want (see more on this in my book *The Half Lived Life: Overcoming Passivity and Rediscovering Your Authentic Self*).

Passivity is difficult to identify because one of the greatest tricks a passive man plays on himself goes something like this: "Look how hard I work. I work eighty hours a week and am the CEO of a large company. How can anyone label me as passive?" or "Look how much I work on myself. I go to five twelve-step meetings a week and see my therapist regularly; how can I be passive?" "Can't you see I'm suffering? Isn't that proof that I'm not attached to passivity?"

One of the greatest tricks I played on myself and Grace is "Look at how busy I am; who would ever identify me as being passive?" I was most passive in the areas of work and money. I used an extreme amount of work to keep me from engaging Grace emotionally at the level I might have been forced to do if I hadn't been gone from home 200 days a year. I was almost equally passive regarding my finances. I never really monitored them carefully, and I didn't know what my expenses were because my assistant would take care of those. I didn't even know if I had enough money to buy the farm in Asheville. Grace, who was very money conscious regarding saving and paying off bills, wanted to pull her hair out (or pull my hair out!) because of my passivity toward money.

One of the main symptoms of passivity is being out of balance in our personal and professional lives. Many reading this were thrown off balance even as babies when our wounded mothers looked in our eyes for comfort and relief. The passive person's creed is, "I'm feeling overwhelmed," or they feel that too many people need them or that they themselves are too needy. They think the world acts on them and moves them rather than being actors and movers themselves. It is important to note that passivity causes you to react rather than act, control rather than respond, manipulate rather than make, or self-destruct instead of create. The passivity I am discussing is not to be confused with passive-aggressive behaviors: timidity, shyness, apathy, or laziness. It is also not to be misconstrued as surrendering or letting go, "turning it over," or practicing passive resistance. All of these are very active processes that actually energize the ones doing them. The passivity discussed here is more akin to giving up, feeling hopeless, feeling defeated, settling for, or feeling unsatisfied. The man who is over-attached to his mother may feel all of these, and he may have witnessed great degrees of passivity in his mother/father. Remember, children don't take after strangers.

MOVING PAST PASSIVITY

By working with your tendencies to be passive, especially in relationships, you are taking the first critical step to take your life to the next level, a level that is more emotionally rewarding and satisfying. Unfortunately, many people have developed a greater connection to loss and feeling less than; they settle for unfulfilling relationships or careers that never quite allow them to achieve their creative potentials. Surviving rather than thriving has become the state that many are not only used to but are also compelled to pursue. It is this nonengaging that lets life pass you by because you did not have the information and tools to take action to change things for the better. You now have the information and tools. Passivity is a learned behavior, a reaction to life that can be unlearned. Passivity is an offense of omission—not doing or saying what you need to, not responding, not accepting challenges, and refusing to take risks—rather than of commission, and that is one reason it has been overlooked by clinicians and writers.

Passivity compels people to wait in a state of suspended animation until something or some mother-like someone "rescues" them from their current circumstances. This knight in shining armor (whether a person, the world, society, or a supernatural being) is supposed to bring the passive person something he feels he has lost or had taken from him. That something could be hope, energy, love, trust, faith, the perfect job, an unconditional lover, the winning lottery numbers, or the good parent he never had, once had, or wished he had. It is a psychological, physical, emotional, and spiritual condition that plagues even the most educated and self-directed people; therefore, the whole person must be addressed. Once it is, you can move from passivity to pursuing your life passions and your relationships rather than seeking your mother's approval or validation.

Exercise for Sons and Partners

Mothers are also invited to participate. Take a few moments, and on a sheet of paper or your computer, answer the following questions as honestly as you can:

- What walls are still in place in your life, and with whom?
- What are you still pleading for and to whom?
- What would you have loved to do but are still blaming someone else because you haven't done it?
- What are you getting out of your passivity today?
- What does your passivity cost you today?

The following four assertive statements will help bring you out of your passivity:

1. I want _____

_____

_____

_____.

2. I need _____

_____

_____

_____.

3. I will not do this to get the above wants and needs met, achieved, or accomplished: _____

_____

_____

_____.

4. I will do this to get these wants and needs met, achieved, or accomplished: _____

_____

_____

_____.

Chapter 4

Appropriately Expressing Anger About the Mother-Son Dynamic

MY MOTHER WOULD BE A FALCONRESS AND I, HER GAY
FALCON TREADING HER WRIST, WOULD FLY TO BRING BACK
FROM THE BLUE OF THE SKY TO HER, BLEEDING, A PRIZE.
—*Robert Duncan*

Dismantling the Mother-Son Dynamic takes a man into
his body and through his losses at points and places along the
way. He'll confront the fact that if his mother had been there for

him less or more as a boy, adolescent, and young man, the bumps, bruises, and abuse he'd received and perpetuated would have been fewer and farther between. When a man feels his mother abandoned him or smothered him, he will feel anger and grief.

When boundaries are violated and emotional incest, or abuse of any kind, occurs, a natural and healthy response is the expression of appropriate anger. For the first three decades of my life, I devoted myself, body and soul, to caring for my mother. I remember trying to become a minister, not so much because I wanted to, but because I knew that was what my mother believed I had been born to become. I existed only to the degree that she felt satisfied. When I stood on the verge of middle age, I examined my direction in life. For example, had I chosen to be a teacher to satisfy myself and my soul or to plug the hole in my mother's soul?

Not long ago I was in the deepest despair I have been in for some time. The time I had taken off to examine my soul took me into a state of depression, which I define as an inability to feel when it is not biochemically induced. Knowing that I was wrestling with my mother issues, I called my mother for support. My mother, herself in recovery for over four years, has become a great friend and, most of the time, is able to listen without lecturing or trying to fix me. I told her how badly I was doing. Immediately she slid into the role of mother: "Now, Son, God won't put on you any more than you can bear. I'm sure He's put you in this mood for a good reason. Maybe you'll be able to share it with the people who come to your lectures."

I was seized by uncontrollable fury. I yelled into the phone as if I were yelling into the past: "Shut up! Just shut up and listen to me, damn it! You're not listening to me! You're scared of my feelings and my depression, and you're hiding behind your religion. If you want to be a preacher and a teacher, be one, but quit living your life through me. Listen to me telling you how I feel. And if you can't, then say you can't, but stop hiding. I am not the man you need me to be!" As I stood clutching the phone, my head and my heart pounding with rage, I realized that I had never yelled at my mother before in my whole life. To my utter surprise, and despite my angry tone, she heard what I had said and apologized. Silently I apologized to myself for not standing up to her long ago.

When is it appropriate or advisable to confront your mother? Let's say that your body is like a gunny sack full of ten thousand pounds of repressed anger or rage. It is highly unadvisable to go to a mother or a father or anybody until that weight has been reduced significantly, or else everything that will be said will be primarily inappropriate rage rather than an appropriate expression of anger. This was a mistake I made early in my career while writing my first book, *The Flying Boy*. I confronted my father prematurely, not knowing that a great reduction in my rage should have occurred first.

Now, obviously, not every man needs to yell at his mother. Indeed, as I explained in my book *Facing the Fire: Experiencing and Expressing Your Anger Appropriately*, there are ways to express ourselves so as not to threaten or intimidate. For many men, yelling is a way of life. Still, I was raised not to yell under any circumstances, so doing so was a major risk for me. And it was a major accomplishment: I broke a pattern that very much needed to be broken.

I had thought that my mother and Grace were so fragile that they would crumble under pressure from a loud outburst. Having heard my father yell at my mother, I had vowed to keep silent even when a raised voice might have been called for—like when I needed to say "Stop" or "No" or "I don't want you to leave." But this time, when I did yell, I discovered that my mother wasn't nearly as fragile as I'd thought. I learned later that Grace wasn't nearly as fragile as she or I thought. One evening during a heated argument I yelled at her, "I hate your guts." She didn't crumble or die, and though I didn't express anger appropriately, neither of us disappeared. I realized I hadn't wanted to yell because I was afraid Mom and Grace would leave. I needed to see that they wouldn't.

From such experiences, I have come to believe that if you're afraid to tell your mother how you feel, then you tend to turn all other women into mothers, and you won't really tell them what you feel, either. Many men say they want women who will stand toe-to-toe with them, look in their eyes, listen, and speak their truth. But often the same man won't do that with his mom, couldn't do it as a child, and therefore can't really do it with his partner. As long as I was afraid that my mother would be killed by the truth, I was afraid my truth would be deadly to others. Anger is for getting out of stuck places, and Lord knows I'd been stuck a long time.

I was now able to see how anger can help a relationship and make it stronger *if I express it appropriately*. I wanted to learn that anger expressed appropriately equals energy, intimacy, and serenity, as well as what inappropriate anger looked like so I could recognize it before it became hurtful and drove a wedge between my partner and me. I wanted to learn a better way to express anger for my personal benefit, the benefit of my partner, and the benefit of our relationship together.

Let me share my experience with beginning anger work with my Mother-Son Dynamic. Looking back with over twenty-five years of hindsight, I see that I was not only in shock and regressing back to my childhood but I was enraged that others could feel sadness, anger, joy, and love, but I couldn't access these basic feelings.

I chose to see a therapist, Dan Jones (who would become a life-long friend and esteemed colleague), because I had come across his ad in a local health and well-being magazine. It simply said to come see him when and if it was time to deal with anger and sadness and separate or end a relationship. I was experiencing a great deal of depression. I approached his office with a good deal of fear but willingness to try anything or anybody that might help me relieve my pain.

We entered his therapy room that had nothing but carpet and pillows. I found my spot; he found his, and the work on my life began from another perspective. It was work that would last for several months. As Dan and I unfolded to each other, I quickly began to see that this man was not like the other three psycho-therapists I'd seen. In the first session, Dan helped me realize that I was much angrier at nearly everyone and everything than even I had thought, even though the last several months had been filled with recognition of my anger and the occasional ability to show it. The one or two times I had shown my anger I was usually alone, and then able to show it only momentarily. I could not stay with it because I was afraid of it. *What if I lost total control?* (In my work as a therapist, I've since heard that statement by thousands of men and women regarding releasing their anger.)

"How do you feel about your mother, John?" he said.

I told him my story about how she and I were enmeshed and how I was turned into a little adult long before I should have been. I told him how she let me take care of her all those years. I'd bring her cool cloths to comfort her persistent headaches and listen to her sadness by the time I was five.

"But how do you feel about that, John?"

"I don't know." I began crying. I'd been crying for months and then it suddenly dawned on me that one of the reasons I'd cried was because I really didn't know how I felt. I was sad that I couldn't get angry.

"Are you angry at your mom?" Dan gently asked.

"Yes. Damn it, I'm angry!"

Dan grabbed a large pillow next to him and placed it in front of me. "Say 'I'm angry' again and let your fist hit the pillow as hard as you'd like."

"Dan, I don't want to hurt her. She was doing the best she could. She was a lot less abusive than Dad."

"You're not hurting her. But you are hurting yourself by holding in this toxic rage and anger."

I got numb and shut down because my fear was greater in that moment than my anger was. It was my classic symptom of knowing I was angry but not being able to express it. I let my hand fall limply into the pillow. "I'm angry," I squeaked.

"I'm angry!" he said. "Try again, this time really letting go into the pillow. You won't hurt it."

"I'm angry." The pillow was still only lightly touched. "Dan, I can't do this." I grabbed the pillow and threw it to the side. "I can't do this. I can't hit the thing."

Dan didn't force me to hit the pillow. I left his office that first day much more aware that I had a great deal of anger and that I had an even greater inability to let it out. I was scared of what would happen should I get as angry as I really felt. When Dad was angry

I couldn't predict his behavior; therefore, I couldn't control it. The illusion of prediction and control were about all that allowed me to survive my crazy childhood. I still felt a need for both to be secure, though both had contributed greatly to my suicidal tendencies and depression.

I went back to Dan's office a couple of days later, still depressed and still in need of discharging the anger I had denied and repressed for such a long time.

"Take this pillow and put your fist into it. Let your anger out. You're not hitting your mother. You're not hurting her; you're letting your anger out into the pillow, which is a way to stop hurting yourself and a way to stop using valuable energy to hold your anger inside you. You could be using that energy for something else." He smiled and handed me a huge pillow.

"John, just say, 'I'm angry at you, Mom.'" Dan was reassuring with his looks and mannerisms, but I was scared to death.

"Dan, if I let this out I don't know what will happen. I've got to keep a lid on it. If I let it out, won't I just be raging like my father did?" I was afraid of the unknown, even though I'd seen my girlfriend at the time throw things and scream, not hurting anybody and feeling better instantly. I still wasn't sure I wouldn't destroy Dan's room and even Dan. He was sure I wouldn't.

"No, this is an appropriate expression of anger that has been building up inside you for decades. Your mother is not in this is room, and she cannot hear you and you cannot hurt her, so this is appropriate. If you were doing this in front of her and hurting her, that would be rage." He smiled and waited until I was ready.

I began to lightly hit the pillow and under my breath muttered, "I'm angry."

"That's it. Say it so she can hear you."

"I'm angry at you, Mom." My volume increased slightly.

"Again," said Dan.

"I'm angry at you, Mom!" The pillow received a heavy blow. I was still too scared to hit the pillow. Anger was not allowed in my family; it was painful, and somebody usually got hurt when it occurred. I was always taught to hold it in; if you held it in you were somehow stronger than those who couldn't. I had been using my strength to contain my anger for over twenty years; I was worn out, and now it was beginning to come out in a healthy way instead of it leaking out a little at a time on the people I loved.

"I'm angry, Mom." I slammed the pillow hard but still not as hard as I was angry. Blood rushed to my face; my pores opened; sweat dripped from me. I clenched my fists. "I'm angry at you, Mom." My hand came down hard with the words. "I'm angry! I'm angry! I'm angry!"

I beat the pillow with each word. I came alive. Energy flowed through my whole body. I pounded the pillow for fifteen to twenty minutes. I was scared, exhausted, delighted, and energized all at the same moment. I breathed deeply, and my throat felt open instead of its usual tightness.

I finally stopped and looked at Dan. He was still there. I hadn't hurt him. He wasn't afraid. He didn't run away, and his face told me he hadn't rejected me for what I formerly thought to be a ridiculous display of emotion. I was aware that I had consciously, and in front of someone, let myself get out of control enough to get something out I'd wanted to say for a long time. I was finally letting go of the incessant need to hold in my anger. Dan and I kept working on my anger toward my mother during that session. When it was over I felt tired and strong at the same moment. My body and mind had connected.

"I'm exhausted and yet, in a way, I feel great," I said.

Dan smiled. "That's right. And you didn't hurt your mom one bit. As a matter of fact, you may find that if you keep doing this, you and she will get closer in a clear, clean, adult way."

I engaged my anger and rage during several more sessions and found that the more I did, the lighter I'd feel afterward and that I was calmer, more patient, and even, dare I say, happy.

TECHNIQUES FOR APPROPRIATELY RELEASING ANGER

In *Facing the Fire*, I discuss these techniques more in-depth. Not all the exercises will work for you, but that doesn't matter. You are looking for the ones that do, because you will be able to use them again and again.

Breathing

The first thing you did out of your mother's womb was take a weird, wonderful breath. Breathing is the royal road to being in your body and to healing. Whenever I'm feeling nervous, threatened, oppressed, mournful, empty, blue, low, or down in the mouth, I take a couple of deep, full-bodied breaths, in and out, and usually that's enough to bring my spirits back to equilibrium.

Breathing increases the energy in your body and evenly distributes the energy so your brain or stomach isn't outrunning the rest of you. Even your mother told you to take deep breaths and count to ten.

Furthermore, if you're feeling something and you consciously keep breathing, you will be able to stay with that feeling until you've experienced it fully and it passes from you. If you stop or diminish your breathing, you will diminish the emotional experience.

You've probably noticed that people who are afraid to hold their breath don't want to feel the emotion that's overcome them. As children, we would stop breathing and go numb to avoid the pain of what was happening to us. When we stopped breathing, however, we turned ourselves into passive victims. The abuse entered our bodies without our putting up a fight, and because we didn't fight it, it dug further into us. Remember now as you're reading this to take full, deep breaths.

Talking

Thanks to Freud, we are accustomed to the idea that we can deal with our psychological problems by talking them out. The crucial thing to make clear now is that many angers are too strong to be talked out right away with the person who caused them or apparently caused them. Talking can express present anger, but it usually can't handle deeply suppressed anger.

Talking about your anger—present or suppressed—is enormously helpful, provided you do it with a safe person: that is, someone who won't be hurt by whatever you say or try to hurt you for having said it. I continually support men and women to say what they wish they could have said or still want to say to someone else before they confront them with those words.

Writing

Psychologists have done experiments that suggest people who write about their most troubling experiences and innermost feelings may be healthier both physically and mentally than those who don't. James Pennebaker at Southern Methodist University conducted studies in which participants wrote for twenty minutes over four consecutive days. One group of participants wrote about their traumatic experiences, often things they had never discussed before. The topics they wrote on included sexual abuse, suicide attempts, and paralyzing guilt and shame over things they'd done. The other group of participants wrote on superficial topics, like a description of the room they were in.

Pennebaker found that those who wrote about their traumatic experiences, for several months thereafter visited doctors and psychologists much less often than they had before and significantly less often than the people who wrote on trivial topics.

In another study, Janice Kiecolt-Glaser and Ronald Glaser at Ohio State University found that people writing about traumatic experiences had more T-cells in their blood than people writing on unemotional topics. T-cells help fight bacterial and viral infection.

Another psychologist, Edward J. Murray of the University of Miami, has done a study that suggests that "just writing about emotional experiences . . . seems to produce as much therapeutic benefit as sessions with a psychotherapist."

These researchers believe that autobiographical writing that tells painful truths is healthful for two reasons. Says Pennebaker:

> It reduces the physical and mental stress involved in inhibiting thoughts. But more importantly, writing is a powerful tool to organize overwhelming events and make them manageable. The mind torments itself by thinking about unresolved issues. By translating the experience into language, people begin to organize and structure

the surge of overwhelming thoughts. Once organized, they are easier to resolve.

Writing Exercises

Many of the exercises in this book involve writing for the reasons above. Here are some additional suggestions for writing exercises.

Complete the sentences:

When Dad got angry, he _____

_____.

When Mom got angry, she _____

_____.

When I got angry as a child, I _____

_____.

Write about a time you were abandoned. Or write about a time you felt smothered. For this exercise, if you're right-handed, write with your left hand. If you're left-handed, write with your right hand. Writing with the opposite hand will get you out of the logical, dominant side of your brain and into the dream side, where your emotions are. If you're right-handed and you write with your right hand, you're likely to write works that justify and rationalize your pain. Your left hand is more likely to speak from the gut. Our opposite hands usually speak for the child in us.

Don't worry if your writing is sloppy. You're the only one who sees it. Breathe and relax as you're writing. Don't try to rush through this exercise; it will take time for your opposite hand to do this unaccustomed task. Let your hand talk to you.

Journal Keeping

Begin a journal. And tell the truth in it!

When journaling, most people present themselves as they want to be seen, as though somebody else were going to read what they wrote. Journal writers realize that what they write isn't going to be read right away—maybe not until they're dead. But still! What are people going to think *then*? The writers want to have their best faces on.

It is *very* hard to get over our need to appear good in other people's eyes, especially our mothers'. Remember that young man in the café who didn't want his mother to know he curses? Psychologists estimate that more than one-third of people in psychotherapy never reveal things about themselves that trouble them because they don't want to alienate their therapists. It is surprising that private journals share the same censorship, but they do. If journaling is to be of real use to us in understanding our emotions, we have to break through the masks of propriety and "good taste" to the feelings that seethe beneath.

PHYSICALLY EXPRESSING ANGER

Sometimes words can't express what we feel. Sometimes the body wants to be heard and the brain to shut up for a little while. Remember, anger expressed appropriately where no one is hurt equals energy, intimacy, and peace of mind.

Scream in the Car

Get into your car, roll up the windows, and scream as loudly as you can. How long should you scream? As long as you have the energy.

If you don't have a car handy, scream into a pillow. You can do this in an apartment, and the neighbors won't hear.

When you're screaming in a car or into a pillow, it is completely appropriate for you to say *anything* you need to get your anger out. Use blaming, hurtful, or accusatory words, obscenities, curses—whatever. Name names. "Mom, I'm so mad at you!" "Son, grow up and be a man!" Verbally expressing violent feelings gets them out of you for the moment and, no less important, reminds you that they are *in* you and that you must recognize the dark side of your nature.

You, of course, understand that you must not say any of these things near somebody who might be hurt by them.

Twist a Towel

Take a bath towel in both hands and twist it as tightly as you can. As you twist your anger into a towel, let out any sighs, moans, or grunts that come up. Or repeat, "I'm angry!" Remember, movement creates emotion.

Imagine the tension in your body being discharged through your arms and hands into the towel. When you finish, the towel will have knots in it that used to be in you and now are not. This is a good exercise if you store anger in your shoulders, neck, hands, and arms. If you store anger in your jaw, bite the towel as you twist, and growl.

Punch a Pillow

Punch a pillow—or a punching bag. And while you do it, talk and curse and moan and yell. The sounds you let out are very important, because they help articulate the preverbal anger and pain you carry from deep in your childhood.

Punch with all the energy you can. If you are angry at a particular person, vent your rage and anger physically. This will feel contrary to all the "decent" ways of behaving you've been taught. You will feel as if you are betraying the relative or friend.

In fact, though, the real betrayal happened long ago, when the person wronged you or left you or disappointed you, a helpless child who knew only that you had to be loved and accepted. You will be discharging into a pillow or punching bag so that you can stop doing violence to yourself by holding in poisonous anger and hatred.

You are not hitting a person. You are hitting the ghost of that person—a ghost from the past, a ghost alive in you that must be exorcised in a concrete, physical way.

Go Outdoors

The outdoors is a great place to express your anger. Go into the woods. Throw rocks. Beat branches against the ground or a boulder or a dead tree. Behave wildly, irreverently. Remember, these are "just feelings"—you're trying to push the savage in you up to the surface and out.

When you're finished, you'll feel more serene, relaxed, and at home in yourself. The savage in you having been eliminated for the moment, you will feel no more than appropriate anger in an anger-producing situation.

GRIEF: MEN'S HIDDEN EMOTION

Dark river beds down which the
eternal thirst is flowing, and the fatigue is
flowing and the grief without shore.
—Pablo Neruda

Grace and I were in the final stages of saying good-bye. But for the life of me, I couldn't let go. She had already found a small apartment by the University of Texas campus, where we were living after we returned from North Carolina. We were still having dinner together and occasionally making love, knowing that it was all coming to an end very soon. One morning during this time, I woke up with the greatest pain in my back I've ever had, before or since. I knew intuitively what was causing the pain and what would relieve it. However, I went against my intuition and went to my wonderful chiropractor, Dr. Angela Bumstead. She saw me, my face contorted in sheer misery and unable to stand upright, and said in her usual caring way, "What do you think this is all about?"

"I know what it's about and what I need to do, but I don't want to do it."

"Do you mind telling me what it is you don't want to do?" Dr. Bumstead said.

"No, I trust you completely," I said. "I have to let go of Grace. Now, please, adjust me and make this pain go away."

I went to see Dr. Bumstead three times that week, but it was beyond her human power to help.

After three sessions with her, I found an acupuncturist in Austin. I went to him, and he asked, "Do you have any idea what is causing you so much pain?"

"Yes. I have to let go of the woman I love. Now, can you stick some needles in me and make the pain go away?

Needle-less to say (excuse the pun), Eastern medicine was not working on this Western man's pain.

This Western man then went to a Western physician, an orthopedic doctor. He didn't bother to ask me if I knew what the pain was about. I went ahead and told him. He looked bewildered and said, "Let's do an x-ray."

The x-rays came back, and he couldn't find anything wrong. By now, this debilitating pain had gone on for two weeks and I could barely stand and walk. Finally, I walked—no, I practically crawled—into the office of my therapist (Sandra Enright at the time). Like Dr. Bumstead and the acupuncturist, she asked, "What do you think this is about?"

And like before, I admitted, "I know what this is about. I gotta let go of Grace."

Sandra knew Grace and me very well, having worked with us for some time trying to stitch this loosely threaded relationship back together again. "I want you to lie down on your stomach on the floor," she said.

I did, completely knowing I was safe in her hands. She asked me to point to where my back was in spasm. She put those loving hands exactly on that place, and I screamed, cried, yelled for about forty-five minutes, "Grace, I've got to let you go!"

After that wrenching session, I got up, standing straight, literally and figuratively, for the first time in quite a while. I walked out of Sandra's office no longer in pain and went to Grace's apartment, where she and I said our final good-byes.

Grief is often the doorway men and women have to walk through to bring them to the point of true departure from a painful or dysfunctional situation and into a whole other life. I grieved some more; Grace grieved some more. Grace entered graduate school, got her master's degree, and became as good as any therapist can be. And I knew, even with the little graduate school I had behind me, that I would never ever marry my mom again.

Men (and women) can repress sadness, hold it in, and cling to it because it may be the last form of connection they have to their mothers or lovers. Many men rage so they won't look so vulnerable. They create the temporary illusion that they are the one in control.

Many men and women fear sadness and grief because they are afraid if they succumb to their sorrows, the black dog—depression—will devour their minds and hearts. Part of why this fear is so prevalent is that we have confused grief with self-pity, which, if participated in long enough, will turn into depression. It will also depress the people around us, eventually leaving us alone in a dimly lit place with only a glass of beer, playing too many "somebody done somebody wrong" songs on the radio in our minds.

Doing grief work is especially difficult for those of us in the West because our culture does not supply the ritual support we need. Taking full responsibility is not without its share of pain. And in our culture, we are afraid of any process in which pain might arise, because we have never been taught that pain can lead to healing. As the African teacher and writer Maladome Some put it, "Emotional pain is the result of resistance to something new—something toward which an old dispensation is at odds."

Growing up, many people—particularly men—were taught implicitly and explicitly to deny what their bodies feel, both physically and emotionally. If you received shame, or an injury like a whipping or beating, or an icy cold, unresponsive stare from a mother's silent face as a child, you probably went numb from the neck down. Any boy subjected to such abuse will try to disappear and will usually fly up into his head, where he'll hide till it's safe to come out. Abuse after abuse leads him to form intellectual and psychological armor against emotions and feelings. By disconnecting from his body, he avoids feeling the whipping or the shame. Numbing the body is the way most of us survived our childhoods.

Frozen inside, we peer out and look at the people walking up to us to be loved or just to give love. Most people use the body to express love, but we can't feel ours for fear the emotions we carry will overwhelm us and others around us, like they did when we were being absorbed into our mothers' bodies and souls.

Two bodies move close to each other, but a man who has been hurt steers his body from behind his eyes. He stops breathing when love is near. Those who "loved" him were those he most feared; they were the ones who threw everything at him from criticism to cheap china to punches.

He holds his breath until the pain stops. But the pain never really stops until we let ourselves breathe, until we decide it's safe enough to let down our guard and give our hypervigilance a rest. We thus hold our bodies up more by our will, rigidity, and fear than by our bones, muscles, and spinal cords.

The wounded son, when told to relax and rest, looks at you as if you're crazy—knowing that you don't understand. When told to let out his anger, rage, and sadness, he points to his body and says, "I can't feel a thing."

For many boys, physical movement was relegated to gym, where we were taunted, teased, and popped with wet towels. The whole educational system of that time, both secular and religious, was at pains to deliver us from our "primitive" impulses, the natural rhythms and needs of our bodies. The act of lovemaking was spoken about in whispers or as a competition of sport, or it was openly reviled, depending on who was doing the talking. Only the brain and the spirit were to be worshipped, elevated, and educated, while the body's wild energies were left to wither. From the beginning it was a hopeless task. Where did our brains and spirits exist, if not in the body? And how could we hope to learn anything if *all* ourselves—the muscle, the mind, the mystic—were not working together as equals?

We all know the rest of this story of imbalance: our beautiful physical beings and our vibrant, leaping energies huddled in the background as our brains conducted us to excellence, achievement, and early heart attacks. "I think, therefore I am" became our battle cry. We said it to ourselves as we slumped, exhausted, in our chairs at the end of the day.

When I ask men in my workshops, "How do you *feel*?" the answer is, "I don't know, I've never really *thought* about it." We say we want to tell people, especially lovers, what we feel, but we've cut ourselves off from our bodies so completely that we've forgotten what feelings feel like! We can't think our way to our feelings any more than we can leap without legs across a stream.

The insistent archaeologist within us demands that we detect our tension, stress, and distress and trace them back to their origins. As Marion Woodman, a Jungian analyst and figure in the feminist movement, observes, "Powerful emotions are locked in our bodies." If we do not discharge the pressures stored in our muscles and tissues, in our backs, faces, throats, and bellies, in our arms and legs, then the energy gets stuck. When we don't release these tensions, we often end up in a breathless effort to talk them out or write them out, when it would have been easier to stretch, sigh, shout, punch, or dance them out in the beginning.

last blow by saying, "because I loved you so much." Still another man sat in the middle of a circle of a dozen other men and wept for many minutes, a storm of tears that represented a childhood, a lifetime.

Of all the ways I know to get our bodies back, to become intimate, and to let people in, the process of grieving is most effective. Men who can grieve, men who can wail in the night, will be able to dance at dawn. As the poet Rumi says, "The cure for the pain is the pain." If they can learn to feel their pain, they will stop projecting it onto women, and they can feel the pain of others without becoming responsible for it or having to fix it.

So many men are reluctant to hold their mothers accountable for the imbalanced, even abusive, relationship they had as mother and son. As my mom said to me after a six-month-long break in our communication years ago, "I've been doing some thinking and realized you have lots of anger towards me." My mouth dropped open for a month. But make no mistake, in order to heal, it must be appropriate anger and not raging at the woman, if she's still alive. The person whom men are angry at the most is the "Ghost Mother"—the mother who didn't know better.

Men who say they don't need to grieve and learn to express anger are fewer in number than they used to be, as society has slowly begun to change in what is accepted as being a man and what is masculinity. Moving into a deeper masculinity cannot be

Date due: April 7, 2016 1 PM

Total checkouts for session
Total checkouts: 3

To check your card and re items, go to
www.calgarylibrary.ca
or call 262-2928

EMBARKING ON
THE JOURNEY OF GRIEF

After you've allowed yourself to get angry about your mother not meeting all your needs—perhaps after you've been raging about it for years—you can continue the process by grieving. The following model of grief can be applied to all issues that arise as you continue your examination of your Mother-Son Dynamic. Ninety-eight percent of the time, anger and grief go hand in glove. Anger is for getting out of stuck, dead-end relationships. Grief is for having been stuck so long.

One way to become more whole is to no longer turn people, substances, or work into our mothers, and to perform the necessary rituals of separation and preparation for individual life. The form of these rituals depends on the culture we come from. Because our culture has so few rituals, we may have to look outside it to find ceremonies and rites of passage that, properly done, will usher a man into his full masculinity and a woman into her femininity.

The ritual aspects of grief work, if done well, can serve Western men in lieu of more formalized ceremonial practices. Grief work has many forms, but basically it boils down to the following: Stop using all drugs—work, alcohol, drugs, food, sex, and television. Spend some time alone and go into the wounds that have been waiting a lifetime to be tended to. Instead of pumping quarters into a jukebox and listening to songs telling you you're no good without a woman, pick up the phone and call a friend for support. Join a men's group in which you tell them about the pain you've found inside, about the terror you feel at the thought of saying good-bye to the mother you never had and never will have. Let the tears run out of your eyes and over your whole body until they soothe your soul and cleanse your wounds. Do this every day, every month, and every year until you don't have to do it any more—that is, until you discover another layer of grief and you begin the process again.

Don't let anybody talk you out of your pain. Don't let your mother, your friends, or the media interrupt your detoxing from the addiction to the patterns that have perpetuated your pain. Write, weep, and wail into the sky in the middle of the night. Sweat, vomit, and excrete your pain. Promise yourself that you'll stop clinging to what you've known—the repression, the addictions, the denial—and go where the wound is. And ultimately go where the healing waits, along with all its attendant fear of the unknown. As you perform this ritual, something you longed for that you some-times got a glimpse of returns. You'll increasingly feel at home in your own skin, a goal most of us want to achieve.

Performing this kind of grief work, we stay in our responsible adult selves (instead of making ourselves into children or some-body's parent, or always worrying that someone will treat us as a child or parent). We feel each moment deeply. We become able to embrace many of the magical possibilities we had as children.

PRACTICING A FOUR-STEP MODEL OF GRIEF WORK

Grief is a normal and natural response to loss.
It is originally an unlearned feeling process.
Keeping grief inside increases your pain.

—Anne Grant

Over the years I have been asked many times, "How do you start grieving the mother-son wound, and what does it look like, sound like, and feel like?" Grieving is different for everyone, but here are a few things that are generally true for most.

Step 1

A person must become conscious of the necessity to grieve all their losses of any kind, no matter how big or small and no matter what anybody tells you or thinks. A person has to mourn not only the loss of things, people, places, pets, stages, transitions, and changes but also everything they wanted but never got. This is a loss to be mourned, as was the case with James.

James is a data entry processor who told me how his mother married for the second time and had a child with his stepfather. She then devoted all her attention, support, and nurturing toward his half-brother. "She always took his side. Even on her deathbed she wanted him there and not me. She even refused to tell me anything about my real father."

We must also completely reject the toxic teachings that have become worn-out clichés concerning genuine grief work: *It's just water under the bridge. Let sleeping dogs lie. No use in crying over spilt milk. Get over it. Get back in the saddle. Pull yourself up by the bootstraps. Keep a stiff upper lip. The past is dead and gone.* As William Faulkner, the great Southern writer, said, "The past isn't dead, it's not even the past."

Step 2

You must develop a support network of people who will stand by you while you are grieving. These are friends, family, a therapist, God or another higher power, a sponsor, or all of the above—the more, the better. These people will not hurry you, shame you, or talk you out of your grief. Rather, they'll let you know "We're here and we know grieving can be scary; that's why you shouldn't do it alone." In other words, use your community to hold your hand while you walk through what can feel like the "valley of the shadow of death."

One of the main reasons we put off grieving is that we have been told not to show our feelings; thus, we believe grieving should be a solitary act, if experienced at all. However, grieving was never meant to be done entirely alone.

A tribe in the Polynesian islands provides the best example of how grieving is a community job. When someone in the immediate family dies, it is everyone's job in that family to mourn and grieve the loss for a full year. During that year, tribe members take care of the children, the garden, the home, the cooking, and the cleaning for the grievers. At the end of the year, the grief cycle is completed because that was their sole—and soul—focus. The family then resumes the business of life.

Step 3

Create a grief ritual. For example, it may be necessary to set aside time each day or once a week or whatever is appropriate for you. For instance, you may get up thirty minutes early before going to work and take your ex's picture out, light some candles, put on what was your favorite music as a couple, and look at the photograph. Tell her how you feel and what you loved and hated about your togetherness, and then weep, wail, get angry, or do whatever. Then get up, take a shower, and go to work.

Roger, an energetic man in his late sixties, once helped organize one of my workshops in South Dakota. He had been a professor of English at the university there for thirty-five years and had recently retired. As we were driving to the campus auditorium where I was to speak, he pointed to a building and said, "See the last window on the corner of the fourth floor? That was my office for thirty-five years."

"I bet there is a lot of you still in that room after all those years," I said.

He then said something I'll never forget: "Not an ounce."

I was taken aback. "How is that possible after all those years?"

"I listened to your tape on grieving, and I did what you suggested because I didn't want any of me floating around in that building when I left. I wanted closure, so when I started my new life, I had completely said good-bye to my old one and honored it in the best possible way I could. Every Friday for a whole year I would sometimes have my students in for little get-togethers. Other times I had my faculty friends over for drinks. Some Fridays I just sat alone in my office and recalled some of my fondest memories. But every Friday I did something to say good-bye to my office, my profession, my students, and my friends, and at the end of that year, I was just full of gratitude for the time spent there."

Most people do not participate in ritual grief work like Roger had. Neither are they able to plan for the need to grieve. Instead, what most do—if they do anything at all—is what I call hit-or-miss grieving. They will start and stop and catch-as-catch-can. They will do a lot for a day or two or a week then convince themselves they are finished; or some idiot—sometimes their therapist or sponsor—tells them they "should be done" and move on. Or they might go to a grief workshop and do a whole weekend's worth. I don't think your twenty-year marriage or your one-year relationship can be grieved in a weekend, and the only person who will know when you are done is you. Remember, a ritual is something you do over and over again until it is no longer necessary. Some last for weeks, months, years, or a lifetime. Most grief rituals for deep, long-standing, or cumulative sorrows usually take six months to a year.

After the work I did with Dan Jones, he and I became colleagues and partners in the teaching of a program we developed, The P.E.E.R. Process (Primary Emotional Energy Recovery). We taught emotional release work, anger work, grief work, and more to several thousands of people in workshops, classes, and experiential therapy. Based on my own experience and Dan's and my experiences with hundreds of people with their grief work, he and I agreed that if a man's grief of the woman he loves is separated from his previous life's sorrows and separated from his mother's grief he often unwittingly carries, he can usually perform a ninety-day grief ritual like the one I will share with you shortly.

This process is much like when an alcoholic first goes into recovery. In twelve-step groups, it is strongly suggested that in the very beginning of recovery a person should attend ninety meetings in ninety days. Although this is a typical amount of time, depending on what grief work you have done in the past and what you are still carrying inside you, your own ritual may continue much longer.

Step 4

I've found it important to have a ceremony at the end of the grieving process. This can be done by, for instance, inviting your friends who stood by you to someplace special—your favorite restaurant or park—and thanking them for the support they gave. This will let them and you see that you navigated the treacherous waters that flowed in your body's ocean of grief. Do you remember Alice in Wonderland? The only way she could get through the huge locked door was to cry and cry, and pretty soon she raised herself on her own river of tears and floated right through the keyhole to the other side of the door—and the other side of her life.

How will you know it is time to do the ceremony? Because you will be in a place to celebrate the time spent between you and the person or thing you've been grieving. You'll be able to praise your mother—past and present—and yourself for all the gifts you gave each other and all the lessons you learned; you will focus on the good parts of your mother. The pleasant memories of your parents are likely to surface, and even the good things you learned from your ex can magically appear. Like Roger, you will find yourself feeling gratitude for the time spent in whatever relationship it was that is now over, and there will be no residual grief, anger, or resentment. Instead, you will bless the person, place, or situation. These are all signs that you have successfully come through this time of loss or change. However, if you are still angry, sitting in some bar drinking and telling the bartender or a stranger that the divorce papers were finally signed and now you are "rid of the bitch," or how much you hated all those years at your job, you're not done—you probably need to go back to Step 1.

To illustrate some of these elements, let me describe a period of grieving I did. I had done my first emotional release work with Dan while I was writing my first book, *The Flying Boy*. At that time, years before Grace, I began to grieve the loss of one of my most powerful loves, Laurel. Since I had never done any grief work before, the loss of Laurel opened a window in me through which I pushed out all the grief that had been unrecognized, unrealized, and unspoken since I was born. Out of that window flowed grief regarding the loss of my high school sweetheart, the loss of a father, the sadness of alcoholism, and the anger of the brutal physical abuse I experienced in childhood. My lifetime of grief of all these things continued to pour out of me for a full nine months of regular work with Dan. By the time I said good-bye to Grace, however, the major part of my grieving process took only roughly ninety days instead of nine months, since this time I was grieving only my loss of Grace and not a lifetime worth of sorrow. I still missed her and loved her, but the worst part of the grieving was done a few months before we even said good-bye.

There are many ways to perform a grief ritual; this is how mine went. I set aside ninety days to do this, choosing to write in my journal about the pain and the sorrow implicit in the act of saying good-bye. Every morning I woke when it was still dark outside and inside. I went to the kitchen, made a cup of coffee, and sat down to drink it. I took out a small journal and my favorite ink pen. Instead of trying to avoid my pain or distract myself like I would occasionally do throughout the rest of the day, I went into it. I remember details of how our love was when it was new and young.

I remembered the ways I felt, things we did together, minute details of her and of our life together. I roamed around in these painful memories and let tears come into my eyes freely and put the pain onto the page as best I could. Nothing was off-limits during this time. I recalled every little stone in the wall that grew up between us, called up the sorrow of our physical pain and losses as well as our emotional pain and losses. Every day I did this, even when I dreaded going back into that dark, hellish, lonely place in myself. After the ninety days, a great weight had been lifted off my chest. I knew that because I had applied myself to the grieving process I would not be carrying this loss with me into the next phase and stage of my life.

Chapter 5

More Solutions

To some extent, the young man,
each time he leaves a woman,
feels it as a victory, because he has
escaped from his mother.

—*Robert Bly*

Thus far, we have done some work to come out of rage and truly express our anger over having been caught in the Mother-Son Dynamic and grieve our losses, and we are working to overcome any remaining passivity we may have toward seeing this dynamic and working toward healthier relationships. Now we are ready to take a look at some solutions to help us live our lives fully, separately, and independently as adults.

MY SEPARATION SOLUTION:
STOP SONNING

One day in my mid-forties I called my mother and very gently and compassionately said, "Mom, you're fired! I don't need you to be mothering me anymore. I'm in midlife; I have been a college teacher for quite a few years and an itinerant lecturer and speaker for a dozen years. What I need is to create a new adult-to-adult relationship with you if it is at all possible."

My mother was silent for a few moments. "I'm not sure what you mean."

"I mean the time for you to be mothering me is over, and the time for me to be sonning you is over. I have to stop sonning— acting, talking, thinking, and behaving like a boy/son—and treat you with respect as an adult, and for you to talk and interact with me like an adult. So I'm going to take some time away from our past relationship, do some more work, and I'd like for you not to call or write until I think and feel I'm ready to re-engage at a level that is more adult to adult."

"How long do you think you'll be out of touch?" she asked, her voice broken and halting.

"I don't know, but I love you and will be back in touch, I promise." We took a six-month break, and we were both scared.

Jason is another example. He had been reduced to raging tears several times in his weekly men's group, remembering how his mother had never listened to him when he expressed his emotions, how she had wanted Jason only to achieve, not grow or feel. One night Jason decided to call her. He wanted to share what he'd learned about his mother relationship and to tell her about the men's gatherings he'd attended. He needed his mom to hear him.

"Well, that sounds fine, Son. I'm sure it was worth the time and money you spent. But I will always be your mother no matter what that therapist tells you. Is he even licensed?"

His mother's patronizing tone and lack of interest put Jason right back where he was before all his work; at least for the moment, he became a son seeking the approval of a mother who couldn't give it twenty-five years ago and still can't.

As Jason told us how much he had wanted his mother to listen, he looked at me with eyes as sad as anyone's I've ever seen and said, "I've even got to let her go at this level, too, don't I? I have to let my mom go, don't I?" All letting go truly means is shutting the tap from which dysfunction flows. There is no therapeutic process that can take away the good stuff your mother gave you. The good memories sometimes are turned on in direct proportion to how much of the bad we let go. Remember, letting go doesn't mean you stop loving, stop caring, or even stop communicating or visiting. It means letting go of the patterns that hold people in place. It means seeing and hearing people as they are, not as they were. It means discharging them from being your sole, or soul, reason for living.

At that instant, I could feel that Jason was finally willing to stop sonning, and he joined the ever increasing group of men who are no longer willing to act on their need for mothering or fathering from their parents. When I then asked Jason to tell his mother how he now felt, he said, "Mom, I'll always be your son and you'll always be my mother, but I don't need parenting by you anymore. I need to stop sonning you. I need you to talk to me like an adult you respect and appreciate. I don't need your money, your advice, your shaming, your criticizing, or for you to ignore my boundaries. I need to treat you like someone who I love and share a great deal of history with. But I need to forge a new relationship with you and I need for you to be willing to try to be my friend as I am willing to try to listen to you and speak my truth, even if it hurts you to hear it."

Jason and his mother are now sending texts back and forth every month or so. They have agreed to use this medium as a way to show each other who they are now. They're trying to become friends.

Once an adult son and his mother can break the pattern of son-ning, this can also help release him from the grip of other patterns he may be playing out in his other relationships (romantic and nonromantic), such as rescuer/rescued and "when you do, I do." In other words, everybody wins, even the mother, if she's still alive. She's got a man in the house or in her life as opposed to a little boy who needs to be taken care of for the rest of her life. I can't tell you the number of fifty- to eighty-year-old women (and fathers) who have said to me, "I wish my grown children could find some way to let me go in a way that's healthy and functional," because at this stage, they don't really want even a part-time job of parenting thirty-, forty-, or fifty-year-old adults.

FOR MOTHERS

We've taken a look at many dysfunctional patterns that can happen between mothers and sons, and now it's time to take a look at some examples of good mothering. The following list includes some examples of how a good mother looks, sounds, and behaves.

A. "I'm glad you are here."

B. "I see you."

C. "You are special to me."

D. "I respect your boundaries and know you are not me and I'm not you."

E. "I will mirror back your radiance."

F. "I will keep you safe."

G. "I will not take the energy from you."

H. "I am a safe place for you when you fall."

I. "If you fall, and you will, I will be there to pick you up until you are an adult, and then I'll try to be supportive."

J. A good mother will know when to speak and when to remain silent.

K. She will know how not to give unsolicited criticism.

L. She minds her own business most of the time.

M. She always treats her adult children like adults.

CEASING TO RESCUE AND SEEK RESCUE

During our years together, Grace and I discovered what worked for us as a solution—a way to break out of the relationship-threatening pattern we were in: rescuer/rescued. What we discovered is hard to explain but necessary to understand. Perhaps the point is best made through a story.

In the film *Fearless*, the main character, played by Jeff Bridges, survives a horrible plane crash. He saves several people's lives and becomes a hero. But something happens to him. He cannot connect or communicate with his wife and child. His primary relationships degenerate while his new relationships with those he had saved take on mystical importance.

Bridges's character slips further and further into the role he never sought, never wanted. He is not sure how to break out. By the end of the movie, he stumbles upon the answer. His wife realizes she must rescue herself and her son from their situation. In an act of desperation she asks her husband what he needs to come back to earth, to his family, to the reality of everyday life.

He looks at her, and with tears in his eyes and desperation in every line in his face, he says: "I need someone to save me."

Now, the irony that this poignant moment shows is that to become fully real, to become fully grounded, heroes need the experience of being rescued from themselves. I was blessed with such a moment when I reached the point of utter exhaustion, having tried to rescue one too many damsels in distress. For the hero in *Fearless*, the moment comes in an elegant, almost Zen-like way. By mistake, he eats a strawberry, which gets stuck in his throat and throws him into an allergic fit. He is in danger of dying; his life as rescuer and savior flashes before him. Suddenly he, too, is a victim of forces he cannot control. His wife rushes in to rescue him, forcing the berry out of his throat, and in so doing forces out the demon that had been driving him to rescue others. At that moment he is able to allow the people he loves to come into his heart. He once again sees and reconnects to the ordinary world by stepping out of a dysfunctional, albeit heroic, role.

When I was a rescuer, I found I could easily create intimacy with anyone as long as he or she didn't get too close, become too primary or important. The people I let myself get close to had to be rescued; not only that, I had to live with them. What kept us together? Resentment.

In a dream I am swinging on a vine over a sparkling lake. I am playing like the child I never got to be because I was always too busy being the family rescuer. In the dream I am aware that I am a full-grown man having fun and delighting in this boyish energy. I can swing all the way to the other side of the lake any time I want. In the middle of my delight I see a hand rise out of the water—it is a woman drowning and making her last effort to signal someone to rescue her. I make my usual decision, letting go of the vine and plunging into the lake. I dive through the water but can't find the woman. Finally I summon all my energy and dive deeper. Suddenly I discover an underwater cave. I enter the cave, and there I see the woman. But instead of being in peril of her life, she is calmly breathing the air trapped inside the cave. I realize she was not drowning at all. Instead, she merely comes out of the cave periodically, trying to signal someone to help her out of the cave of helplessness.

When I awoke from this dream, I analyzed it the way I've been taught. I read each part of the dream as something about myself. But for the first time I did something I'd never done. I interpreted the dream as being about Grace and me: me the rescuer, Grace the woman who appeared to be drowning but was actually breathing in her cave. I told Grace that I was ready to give up my role as hero and rescuer. I wanted her to see that she didn't need rescuing any-more, and that I wanted her to come out of the emotional cave she had formed in childhood and still often hid in during our relation-ship. From this dream I saw that in playing my role I, too, had been in a cave of sorts; that by rescuing I was throwing away the energy

I needed to play and have fun. I needed the energy to swing to the other side of the lake: the mysterious other shore, where I'd never allowed myself to go before, where the old patterns are left behind.

Grace heard my dream and my request. She knew that it held a great deal of truth for her. If she comes out of her cave, and if I stop giving up my energy, we'll have a chance; we'll have healing—we'll have a relationship.

If those who have been trained to descend into underwater caves and those who wait to be saved changed our behavior, what would we be like? What would we do with all the energy we suddenly gained? Instead of being emotional divers, rescuers, and spelunkers into someone else's psyche, we would no longer be on call, or find ourselves on white horses, on stage, or continually on guard. We could relax and let the mothers of the world take care of themselves, just as my mother and Grace did when I told them my truths. Remember, rather than being active, rescuing is a passive behavior that keeps one from attaining what he or she really wants from life.

ADDRESSING CODEPENDENCY

As I mentioned before, many patterns in the Mother-Son Dynamic (like rescuer/rescued) stem from codependency. Many varying degrees of codependency exist, and based on the severity of it in any given relationship, it may need to be addressed more directly.

First, one must realize that codependency, no matter how many people make light of it or how the media have caricatured it, is a terminal disease. People die from codependency all the time, but most people do not recognize it to be the killer it is. Codependency is a small or major factor in coronary disease, addictions, depression, and dangerous behaviors with dangerous people. It must be treated as the serious condition it is. Codependents are often called other things, like Saint Mom, a good wife, the salt of the earth, my hero, ultra-new-age and ultra-radical caretakers.

I highly encourage you to make a conscious effort and commitment to recover from this complex and complicated issue. One way to work toward coming out of your codependency is to read, reread, and memorize Melody Beatty's book *Codependent No More*. Beatty wrote, "I saw people who constantly gave to others but didn't know how to receive. I saw people give until they were angry, exhausted, and empty of everything.... Most codependents are obsessed with other people" and "yet these codependents who have such great insight into others couldn't see themselves. They didn't know what they were feeling. They weren't sure what they thought."

You might consider going to a twelve-step program called CODA (Codependents Anonymous) or Al-Anon, which stresses relief from codependency as well. Or you might want to find a therapist who specializes in this issue. They're not as plentiful as they used to be in the '80s and '90s, and you can still find five- to sixteen-day workshops on this issue. If you'd like more information about these, do an Internet search or ask friends or therapists, or ask twelve-step group people.

FINDING NONLIBIDINOUS LOVE

A helpful way to think about and work with anaclitic depression (the kind of depression that comes from never having received love that did not have sexual hints or overtones) is to feel the hurt, sadness, and anger that comes from being a *source* of energy and fulfillment for a tired, drained, or drugged mother, and to let the anger and sadness come out of your body, heart, and soul.

As recounted earlier, when I asked Grace to hold me after my night of bad dreams, there was no transference of sexual energy, no expectation of reprisals or repercussions. She held me from a place in her heart in a way that my wounded mother was incapable of, as my mother herself never received this pure love.

Once this type of depression is identified, a man or a woman must find someone, if not the partner or spouse, to give this non-libidinous love. This very often can come from a mentor, teacher, or good friend. However, the depressed or codependent person has to work hard to let it in.

Make a list of men and women currently in your life who might be able to provide this kind of soothing balm to your sore soul. If you find few or no one on the list, you have to find some new folks and admit them into your heretofore closed heart. Many people who are not extroverts find it difficult to attend social events and gatherings where friends of the same feather may be, so they don't go. This is another form of passivity. Often, men will have only one best friend, if even that. That friend may live five states over, as if there is no one in all of Chicago or Cincinnati or Jacksonville he could be friends with.

Also, if one begins working emotionally at the level on which many of you reading this book are committed to working, you may have to gently let go—or outright fire—friends who may not be supportive of what they may see as a radical departure from your old life. However, with the advent of the Internet, it has become exponentially easier to find people who are interested in the same things and growing in the same direction as you are.

The other night I had a dream. A young woman propositioned me. For twenty-five dollars, she said, she would do anything I wanted. I could see that she was suffering terribly from some unspoken wound. I refused her proposition and offered instead to listen to her tell me what was troubling her. She looked surprised but began to speak. As she did, I began massaging the soles of her feet. An older man and woman appeared in a truck, and I got scared, afraid they'd mistake my intentions and hurt me or her. But they were just concerned about her well-being, as I was, and when satisfied she was in "good hands," they left. I awoke and realized one of the things Grace loves the most is a foot massage. Still, one of the hardest things for me to do is give her one that lasts for any length of time without feeling like I'm slipping away and dissolving into the past where I did things like this for my mother. But now I realized that I was ready to provide anaclitic (caring, nonsexual) love to someone else. I also realized the woman in my dream, whose sole/soul was in my hands was really me, my soul, my feet, tired of walking in search of something that has been inside me all along. I could also receive this beautiful type of love.

MENTORING AS A SOLUTION TO THE MOTHER-SON DYNAMIC

Remember who taught Parsifal to ask the right questions? Gournamond, his mentor.

One way to extract yourself from the magnetic pull of your mother and to develop the inferior functions in your life without placing too much pressure or expectation on your partner is to find a mentor. Young men, old men, men in the middle are almost all in need of a mentor. An ideal mentor is a man (or for a woman, a woman) who can teach, encourage, hold up a lamp during a dark time, model, and make meaning out of chaos. They are not to give what Mom or Dad could not. They give another kind of energy that is not conflicted by history or biology or guilt or shame.

Most men have never had this kind of mentor, or what Robert Bly calls a "male mother." They've never had someone who helps nurture their talents and encourages them to pursue their passions. The mentor's role is not that of father or therapist; a mentor does not feel or heal the younger man's pain. He is there to stimulate his curiosity and provide information and share experiences.

Two men have mentored me in my adult life. They provided information and support I could not have gotten—nor should have expected to get—from my mother or from my partner. Wayne Kritsberg sat down with me years ago after having read my first book, *The Flying Boy*. He recommended it to his publisher and told me some things I could expect being on the road and how much to charge as a speaker. He very carefully and noncompetitively guided me through a process that would have been overwhelming were it not for his information. He wanted nothing in return.

Bill Stott, now a coauthor of two of my books, mentored me in the writing process. For years he would read the words I'd strung together in less than artful ways, commenting on them in constructive, rather than critical, ways. He was supportive of me during those early years when I had little confidence or ability to support myself. He shared with me every secret he knew about good writing. He shared parts of himself and his history I could relate to and use. These men helped me learn and grow in ways my mother or partner could not. Both of these men, along with several others, mentored me in my personal life. It was Robert Bly who encouraged me to always bring home a little gift for Grace when I arrived home from traveling for speaking and teaching engagements.

However, to make mentoring effective, men must not expect their mentors to be anything but the flesh-and-blood beings that they are. Mentors can't and shouldn't be our mamas or saints or saviors. The mentor you select is only too human and is probably still healing his own wounds and recovering at his own pace, just as we are. We cannot forget that we need the mentor's words, his art, his wisdom, and his knowledge, although we have no right to them. If he gives, we are privileged and should be honored. If he withdraws from us, we can only grieve—never demand.

But a man who has not let his mother go, a man who has not stopped being a son, will misuse his mentor; he'll feel abandoned when his mentor doesn't spend as much time with him as he'd like or return his phone calls as quickly as he wants him to. A man still clinging to the mother he never had and always wanted will project his unfulfilled needs onto his mentor.

A time will probably come when we'll have to let our mentors go. Indeed, if the ones we choose are healthy, they will gently push us out on our own. And if they are really healthy, and if time and circumstances allow, they will want to cultivate a new relationship—as a peer or a good friend. But we can't reciprocate unless we heal our mother-son and father-son wounds enough to let our mentors go and allow ourselves to see ourselves as equals, all the while still appreciating them and respecting them for who they are and how they helped.

I hope older men (not necessarily in years but in experience), whether in recovery or accounting or doctoring, will make time to mentor other men. And I hope men who have stopped craving a mother will start asking men to be their mentors, knowing they may get turned down some, maybe many. But someone will eventually come into their lives and say yes and then teach them to trust men, trust their own masculinity, and stop looking for mothers in the eyes of every woman they see.

And women: mothers can teach sons or men many things, but they can't teach or model how to be a *man*! I highly recommend finding a male mentor for your young son. Perhaps you have a male friend in your life whom you can trust with your son. If you have male cousins, uncles, or brothers you know to be safe, conscious men, ask them directly to spend time with your son. You can also explore local programs like Big Brothers Big Sisters of America.

What many people don't consider is that fathers are not meant to be mentors. Fathers are supposed to teach a boy how to tie shoelaces. Mentors are supposed to teach a boy how to tie his dreams to a kite and let it fly. Fathers are supposed to pick up the son who falls off his bike and gets gravel stuck in his knee. Mentors are meant to help the boy whose kite has fallen to earth along with the dreams he tied to it, and give him support to dream other dreams. Fathers are meant to model manhood; mentors are meant to help usher boys into manhood.

Exercise for Men

- Write down the men who come to mind and heart who have mentored you.
- Write down who tried to mentor you but at a time when you weren't ready to receive it.
- What are your fears of being mentored?
- Who are you mentoring or have you mentored, and how did it go?

MEN'S GROUPS AND GATHERINGS

While looking and being open to being mentored, men's groups can be extremely helpful in dealing with the Mother-Son Dynamic. Unfortunately, our society is not conducive to older men guiding younger men. This is one of the things that the late eighties and early nineties men's movement tried to address and did so somewhat successfully. We actually saw fathers and grandfathers bring sons and grandsons to our men's conferences when the boys were eleven or twelve years old. These same men now come by themselves ten and twenty years later. This was a great thing to see.

The important elements in having a men's group are a common commitment to attend regularly, to share, to listen, and to honor the feelings and issues that come up in a safe, nurturing environment. You don't need a therapist to be in a men's group. You just need to be a man who yearns for more men in your life and desires more healing in your relationships with others and the planet. Every time you are honest with another man, the Mother-Son Dynamic is weakened just a little.

In groups and the gatherings, safety is an essential ingredient. In a safe environment, a man's feelings can be experienced and expressed. Participants can receive tremendous amounts of support from us coleaders and the other men in the groups. Throughout my career, I have been a part of countless men's groups in many different settings. In them, I have done my own work on the Mother-Son Dynamic and other issues. I try to cofacilitate my groups and gatherings by being a brother, an elder, and a mentor rather than a therapist—a fellow traveler who has some skills and information that might be useful. In other words, if my own feelings emerge in a group or gathering, they get dealt with right there, if it's appropriate.

In the groups and gatherings, men work hard on issues that include the Mother-Son Dynamic and their relationships with women, other men, children, and bosses. They struggle over their fears about money, death, sex, retirement, dependency, and depression. They mourn lost childhoods and the aging of their bodies. They find their formerly hidden sides themselves, rediscover their bodies and their joy. They learn to trust other men, themselves, and the women in their lives. They allow love to come in. And they are helped to become whole.

So much more than I can communicate here goes on in men's gatherings, men's groups, and men's minds, hearts, souls, and bodies. What I've offered is only one-one-hundredth of the emotion, energy, trust, fear, courage, hurt, and joy that is present or lying dormant and waiting to be released. And I must reiterate that a men's group or gathering doesn't "mend" the wounds. The mending is done by the men, alone or with each other, over time. The gatherings, conferences, and groups are just catalysts that speed and deepen the healing. For more information on this, see my books *At My Father's Wedding* and *A Quiet Strength*.

GROUPS AND GATHERINGS: GENERAL GUIDELINES

I often am asked to describe my approach to men's groups and gatherings. I hope the following will be useful to men looking to establish their own groups, methods, and voices.

Dan Jones and I were partners in facilitating men's groups for years. Before that I'd been a loner all my life. I had lectured and taught at universities by myself and still enjoy lecturing and doing daylong workshops alone, and, of course, writing is a solitary endeavor. But when it comes to working with men, it's just more practical and enjoyable to buddy up with a partner. Two men, shoulder to shoulder, back to back, can see more, hear more, be more. And while there is no such thing as perfect partners, I and the men I work with have a deep relationship that grows richer with each passing year.

Men's groups and gatherings are physical as well as psychological and spiritual. For six years Dan and I worked with ten to twelve men in a group for two-hour sessions. About four to six men in that group would get to "work" on some issue or concern. The work is really about helping the men feel their bodies, their feelings, their pasts, their patterns, and, through experiential processes and support, break out of destructive behaviors that bind and cripple them. The other men in the group vicariously experience what a particular man is working on, and if it restimulates something in them, they will have a turn to "work" next rather than confront or interrupt the man working. In other words, the groups and the gatherings are supportive, not confrontational. We believe we engage in enough confrontation in our daily lives to last a lifetime. Indeed, many of our childhoods were one big war waged between us and some unsupportive person.

Poet and storyteller Robert Bly and I co-led men's conferences, retreats, and workshops for men only (and at times for both men and women) for twenty years. He brought messages, ideas, insights, and awakenings to tens of thousands of men by using myth, fairy tales, and poetry, while I focused on feeling and releasing the emotions we've been stuffing. The conferences were also about cognitive restructuring and reframing, as well as forgiving, grieving, laughing, and sharing the deepest parts of ourselves in the company of men who are willing to be there for us as we are for them.

At some point you'll stand up, maybe at dinner, or wake up one more time at 3:00 AM, and you'll decide from someplace deep in your soul that it's time. Time to do the work we wish we didn't have to do. Read closely the Austrian poet Rilke's take on this:

> *"Sometimes a man stands up during supper*
> *and walks outdoors, and keeps on walking,*
> *because of a church that stands*
> *somewhere in the East.*
>
> *And his children say blessings on*
> *him as if he were dead.*

And another man, who remains inside his own house,
dies there, inside the dishes and in the glasses,
so that his children have to go far out into the world
toward that same church, which he forgot."

Some men's groups are led by competent men who are doing their own work, some by men who ride fads like wild horses blindly going over cliffs. You'll know. You'll feel it in your gut. You'll quickly sense whether or not these groups or gatherings are just macho bullshit run like marine boot camps. If a group or gathering demeans, diminishes, shames, or hurts—get out. Seek a place and a person who by their very being says, "I'm safe. This place is safe. No shaming here."

Exercise for Men

- Write down what you were taught as a boy about "men."
- Write down the name or names of men who betrayed you or hurt you.
- Write down your fears about or resistance to joining or starting a men's group.
- Write down your best-case-scenario men's group.

Some men have long been on the scene to help guide others into not so well-lit places, like poet Robert Bly, who popularized what has been called the Mythopoetic Men's Movement. The emphasis in this part of the movement is on myth, story, fairy tale, and poetry as the main tools, mixed with Jungian psychology.

P oet Robert Bly's best-selling book *Iron John* has a superbly written section about the enmeshment between mothers and sons. The king's son needs to grow up. He needs to find something inside of himself that has been smothered or covered by his mother's love. Many men have a portion of unlived life that has been caged up, possibly for decades. In the story, Bly makes it very clear, not at first, but ultimately, where the key is to that cage that has confined his creativity, his masculinity, his passion, and his purpose. Where do you think this mother's son is to look for that key? Over the years, I've had women working with this issue and men who were conscious enough to work with this issue make all kinds of conventional and otherworldly speculations about where that key might be. Here are some of them:

- In a cave
- In the stars
- In academia
- At their hunting lodge
- In the eyes of every woman they've ever met
- In the heart
- In God
- Through the mystical powers of a shaman

- Under the doormat (Where else is a key kept?)

If you said the doormat, you're actually closer than you think, because it is in the home. Believe it or not, it is under his mother's feather pillow. And no one thinks to look there. I didn't until I was thirty-three years old. I'm sixty-three now, and sometimes I still forget where that key was taken from. And every once in a while, I'll still look under the mat or into a beautiful woman's eyes. But in this myth and symbolically in real life, it's still under the mother's pillow.

The men's movement was and still is an umbrella many are under, and many more are looking for. It's essential that the umbrella remains large enough to shelter all healthy and functional approaches, that we support one another, and that we continue to bring in others of different races and socioeconomic backgrounds.

While we work under this gigantic parasol, we must dialogue and communicate our fears and feelings as we receive the fallout and the hailstones of anger and misunderstanding that are bound to fall on us from time to time. When men get together, the gathering itself can evoke some fear about what is going on, especially if the intent is not to drink or kill something but instead to give life to one another.

Many men come to my seminars and gatherings and then leave to go back to their small towns—or large ones—where they can't find a men's group. The solution: start one yourself. Look inside and see what you love, what you want, what you have to share.

Perhaps you can find one other man, then later two more and then maybe four other men to get together once a week to tell one another your dreams. Or perhaps you like poetry, so you find others to read and discuss how poems make your body hunger, hurt, and heal. Or you might start a men's twelve-step group. The important elements must include a common commitment to attend regularly, to share, to listen, and to honor the feelings and issues that come up in a safe, nurturing environment. You just need to seek out more men in your life and desire more healing in your relationships with others and the world.

SOLUTIONS AND EXERCISES FOR PARTNERS OF MEN IN A MOTHER-SON DYNAMIC

Some women who are reading this book intuitively know or feel that their husbands, boyfriends, lovers, and even fathers have anything from a quirky to an outrageously abnormal relationship to their mothers. And having read this far they may have recognized many indicators that the Mother-Son Dynamic is in play.

What's a woman to do? If you have seen some of the characteristics and behaviors I've outlined in the book, you may have known it when he first introduced you to his mother. You may have felt it when she held on to her son too long at the wedding; you certainly saw every holiday when the son was treated like a prince and the mother as either his queen or his princess.

By now you have either a feeling in your gut or a fear in your heart that you'll never be able to un-know this again. Do you confront your husband? Do you challenge his mom? Or, like most, do you swallow it, bottle it up, seethe, or let it leak out in passive-aggressive ways? As you well know, none of these work. So what does work? You hire a therapist full time to live with your mother-in-law! And then if that doesn't work, you may have to try therapy yourself.

But first, yourself. In direct proportion to how much insight you are able to gain about this issue, the more comfortable you'll be discussing it with the man you love. It is essential to moving forward that women do their anger work and grief work at having been turned into mothers and accept responsibility for their behavior.

What I *don't* recommend is reading this book and then trying to force-feed it to your husband, because that's what mothers do to sons. When you're ready and in your own time, you will more than likely need to have one if not several discussions with the man you think you love or have committed your life to.

WHOMEVER YOU'RE WITH
IS WHERE YOU ARE

I've been saying this to men and women clients and workshop participants for over twenty-five years: "Whomever you're with, that's where you are," meaning that the company you keep (spouses, partners, and lovers included) reflects where you are in your personal journey and growth. You wives, girlfriends, and partners picked this man. You saw the boyish, flighty, handsome, charming mother's son and kept loving him, divorcing him, and marrying him again. Women have told me a hundred times, "I keep falling for the same guy. I keep marrying the same man. What's wrong with this man?"

Like sons and mothers, wives and partners must assume responsibility for changing an unhealthy situation or relationship into a healthier one. One of the places you have to start looking at this issue is how you came to be here. We'll start by briefly exploring your childhood and role models. Women must look at how they were fathered and then determine if they are putting it or the opposite on their husbands, sons, and lovers.

Exercise for Partners

Answer these questions as honestly as you can.

- What do I get from the boy-prince who puts his mother on a pedestal? Do I get a nice boy? Do I get a good ethical man? Do I find my soul mate in this beautiful new-age wonderboy?

- Who was your father? Did you know him? Was he a "mother's boy"?

- What was he like? The opposite of your partner? Or similar? Raging, rugged, and rough, or gentle, sweet, and nice?

Ultimately, neither by itself is satisfying, but in most cases the first model for masculinity is the father, if he was there at all. And if he wasn't, he becomes a negative model. A famous song in the early 1900s had the lyrics, "I want a girl, just like the girl that married dear old dad." Translated, I want the woman my father married. This applies to women tending to marry men just like their fathers, as well as men tending to marry their mothers.

CEASING TO CARRY
THE EMOTIONS OF OTHERS

Women, don't you need to stop carrying emotions for men? What many men and women do is "acquire" rather than access the valuable traits they see in the other person. See if you can relate: My mother unconsciously carried my father's sadness for him, and he unconsciously carried her anger. This was an unspoken agreement between the two. In other words, she was sad enough for both of them, and he was angry enough for both of them.

Women (perhaps not so much the young women of today, but in general) are often the carriers not only of their feelings but of every person's feelings in the house. My sister carried some of my dad's feelings for him. I carried some of my mother's feelings for her. In therapy, as a therapist, one of the hardest tasks I have is to help men and women separate what they really feel from those carried feelings of others. Based on my experience, a woman has to be responsible for her feelings and emotions and let the man she loves or cares for carry his own. As a woman, you may have to give back your mother's or father's feelings, as I said earlier. They are not going to retrieve them. This is an active process that will lighten your emotional heaviness without doing any harm to anyone.

Exercise for Partners

- Make a list of the feelings and emotions you know your mother had but did not have the freedom or the safety to express.

- Have you carried these emotions your mother could not express, or did you act them out?

- Make the same list for your father, and reflect on how you carried and acted out his emotions.

- Are you enmeshed with your partner intellectually, emotionally, or financially? For example, do you let your partner make all the financial decisions while you have no input?

Women must take their inherent power back by pulling out of any enmeshment they have with men, identifying what ways they give their power away: intellectually, emotionally, financially.

BREAKING PATTERNS AND THE ROLES YOU PLAY AS PARTNER

If you are also putting your partner in the same role, or perpetuating the same patterns that play out in his relationship with his mother, this could be exacerbating the Mother-Son Dynamic. This is not an uncommon situation, because men (as women and their fathers) often seek a partner who is similar to their first model of a woman: their mothers.

If you find you are putting him in the same role his mother does and engaging in some of the same patterns, stop. Now that you know what some examples of these behaviors are, you'll be more likely to see and notice when you use them in your interactions with your partner. Then, as you become aware of them, you can do them less and less until you have, for the most part, stopped or at least greatly reduced them.

The same goes for how you behave around his mother. For example, if his mother tries to mother you, you now have the resources to see this pattern and understand why it's important to discontinue it. You can behave as the adult you are.

Hopefully, both of these actions will, either slightly or greatly, reduce the symptoms of the Mother-Son Dynamic. Even if things remain largely unchanged between mother and son, you at least will have gotten yourself out of the triangle with your partner and out of a dynamic with his mother if you had been a part of it.

Exercise for Partners

Next, we'll take a look at your patterns as wife, girlfriend, partner, or lover:

- Do you play any of the roles or share any of the behaviors your partner's mother uses to relate to him? For example, do you mother him? Do you feel like you are rescuing him, or that you are allowing/expecting him to rescue you?

- Do you see any codependent behaviors in your relationship with him? Do you put his feelings and interests and needs before your own?

Once you are spending more time in a balanced adult role in your individual relationship with each of them, you are better equipped to set appropriate boundaries and limits and extricate yourself from this triangle (I'll give you more details on boundaries and limits in the next chapter). To do this, I recommend not talking to your mother-in-law about personal, intimate matters regarding her son and not talking to your husband, boyfriend, or lover about your issues with his mother until you have explored those issues in a more objective or therapeutic manner. You will also know when to depart or deepen, whether in the moment or for longer, and you'll find yourself less angry and less anxious. In other words, when you begin to feel uncomfortable with the dysfunctional Mother-Son Dynamic, you might be able to do anything from taking deep breaths to temporarily removing yourself from the context for five minutes, five hours, or forever if the case warrants it.

Chapter 6

Finding and Maintaining Rhythms of Closeness

How we enter into love and behave in closeness
and nearness . . . [our] habitual structure of
relating, patterns of gesture and tone of voice,
all bear the marks of mother.

—*James Hillman,* Jung's Typology

We've identified the Mother-Son Dynamic in play,
gotten angry, grieved, and begun to find mentors to help us on
our journey. Now our task is to understand what our individual

rhythms are. Not knowing our deep, internal rhythms can be deadly to our relationships with others. How long did your mother stay with you before being called away or before she grew impatient with your neediness? How long could she be with you before she said something shaming that sent you hurling into outer space? How long could she stay before giving way to sickness? How long could she stay with her lover, your father, before disappearing? Her rhythms are embedded in your muscles, tissues, bones, and memory.

Our rhythm of closeness—the "come here, go away" cha-cha-cha that we may have danced with our lovers and spouses—was set by the family in which we were raised. In the same way, movement toward and away from our mothers, and their ability to move into and out of our personal and psychic space, has shaped our ability to allow someone to be close to us or to keep that person at arm's length. For each man this distance is different.

If a mother constantly invades a boy's personal space, he will grow up looking for lovers who want to be so close that they will sleep in his skin and call it love, or he will attract women who will give him much more distance than he can comfortably handle.

If the mother is not there emotionally but uses the boy to fill her emotional void, he'll look for a woman who constantly needs him in the same way. If she leaves him emotionally and physically, he'll be lost. He will appear like the genius Kaspar Hauser in Werner Herzog's film *Every Man for Himself and God Against All*.

This film tells the true story of an unembraced, unwanted, illegitimate child of a European aristocrat and shows how the lack of mothering (and fathering) can affect us. Kaspar lives for two decades in a dark basement without nurturance or love. The only person he knows is a caregiver who brings him food and water and one little toy. Finally, this caregiver, stricken with guilt, takes him out of his black hole of an existence and leaves him in a nearby town. A simple young peasant couple adopts this "adult child" and begins teaching him the basics—how to walk, talk, and eat with a fork. But they can't teach him the most important lesson: how to feel. At one point early in the film, Kaspar approaches the young couple's infant lying serenely asleep in its crib. The viewer wonders whether Kaspar will harm the child because he is unfamiliar with a child's fragility. Just then the mother enters the room. She stops and looks lovingly at Kaspar as he holds the infant with rigid, out-stretched arms. Tears roll down his pale cheeks and he utters the words, "Mother, I feel so far away from everything."

While we are in the womb, our mothers establish the primal rhythm of intimacy; in our infancy, they determine the outward rhythms that will guide our dance through life. How long can a man be with his lover before he feels swallowed up, his energy drained out of him as if someone had pulled the plug on his soul? How long before he runs toward work to escape his inability to be close? It took years before I finally realized that my young father ran to his garage and garden because his rhythms of closeness were very short. Perhaps he could be only as close to his wife and children as he was able to be close to his mother in childhood. And my siblings and I remember our grandmother as cold and distant, never touching and seldom communicative: like mother, like son. Therefore, I often catch myself running toward work as my escape, just as my father did.

FINDING YOUR RHYTHMS

The drummer for the Grateful Dead, Mickey Hart, said, "If two rhythms are nearly the same, and the sources are in close proximity, they will always entrain." For each man to wrestle with the Mother-Son Dynamic, you must discover your rhythm of closeness. How much time can you spend with a lover, wife, or partner before you feel your soul slipping out to sea, before you head for the nearest monastery or mountaintop, or before you buy the newest gadget? How much time do you need alone before you come back to yourself feeling whole again—a month? A week? A day?

Before I understood that I needed to look to my childhood to understand my rhythm of closeness, I tried to discover it by watching and observing other couples. I would look at my friends and think, "They can be together all the time. If I were as healthy as they are, I could spend a lot more time with my partner." But I came to realize that I can entrain to somebody else's rhythms way too quickly, because I had mastered knowing my mother's rhythms by the time I was five or six. I had to come to know and accept the rhythms that are my own.

I must say, I still haven't completely come to terms with my own pace yet. I've realized, though, that I need to be mobile in a relationship, moving in closer or away according to my need.

Sam Keen wrote in his book *Fire in the Belly* that he slept alone one night a week. I thought, "Now, here's a man who knows his rhythms." But suddenly I realized, to my horror and disappointment, that more often than I cared to admit, I needed a week of nights alone. I felt something was wrong with me.

I was still at war with myself about this when Grace and I bought the farm in North Carolina. We were living in Austin, where I'd been for ten years or so. I love Austin, but it's very hot there during the summer, which, despite what the calendar says, sometimes lasts for seven or eight months. Each summer in Austin I swore would be my last. Finally I decided to buy a getaway place where I could beat the heat and write.

For several years I had been renting a little cabin up in the pygmy mountains of northeast Alabama, in a beautiful place called Mentone. Mysteriously cool, it was a hideaway virtually unknown even to the people of Alabama. It was my parents' and grandparents' country; it was my country. Home. The cabin overlooked the valley where my ancestors plowed and where they were buried. I told the owners of the cabin that should they ever want to sell it, to be sure and let me know first. They smiled and said, "You're not the first to ask, or the first to hear us say we'll never sell."

Since the Alabama cabin wasn't an option, Grace and I looked to find something in the Southeast, since we'd both been raised there. Often during the last several years I had given lectures and workshops in Asheville, North Carolina, then a little-known paradise high in the Blue Ridge Mountains. Each time I went I fell more in love with the land there. I felt a peace in my soul that only Southern mountains could provide. Grace and I went to Asheville, looking for a house in the woods to buy, with no luck. On the last day of our weeklong hunt, we were ready to give up when our Realtor showed us a photo of Eden with barns. It was a large home that would need to be a year-round residence, but the Realtor asked us if we'd like to look at it "just for fun?"

We drove past the barn, up the drive, and through the gates. By the time we got to the pond, before we ever even saw the house and guest cabin high atop a hill completely hidden from the road, we were in love with the place. We, and I emphasize *we*—Grace and I—decided to buy it, leave Austin, and move to Asheville. It was a dream we shared of what a place in the country should be. Here we could be happy together and raise, if not children, then horses and sheep and our spirits.

The very day we found the farm and made our plans, I got a call from the owner of the cabin in Mentone. She had tracked me down and called our hotel to tell us that the cabin I loved was for sale if I wanted it. I was forced to confront a deep truth: I loved the cabin in Mentone; Grace did not. But together we loved the farm in Asheville. I opened myself to this new rhythm of closeness.

It's hard to make a short story out of a long-distance move. But it concludes with our living on a farm that became a cauldron of closeness. In this setting, all of our individual and relationship problems emerged, only to be intensified by the heat and lulled into a false sense of security by the cool mountain breezes. And in the bargain I'd lost my ideal getaway place in the mountains of my kinfolk. I made the move because I thought I should be able to live with Grace in one house, in one place, all the time because I loved her and I'd done so much recovery and therapy work.

What I now wish I had done was accept that I needed a place of my own to go, to recharge, recover, rediscover, reconnect, and then return. In buying the farm, even though I loved it too, I was trying to make someone else's rhythms my own. It didn't work. I need a getaway place. I need to sleep alone for a week every couple of months and wander through the woods and write about what I find. Instead of knowing my needs, I tried to second-guess Grace's, and when I did, she and I lost more than we had bargained for. I was doing what I thought I "should" do, being who I thought she wanted me to be: a full-time, all the time, stay-at-home man. But that wasn't what I needed to do. It's not who I was, illustrated perfectly in this poem from William Stafford:

First Grade

In the play Amy didn't want to be
anybody; so she managed the curtain.
Sharon wanted to be Amy. But Sam
wouldn't let anybody be anybody else—
he said it was all wrong. "All right," Steve said,
"I'll be me, but I don't like it."

So Amy was Amy, and we didn't have the play.
And Sharon cried.

Now I can look at my rhythm of closeness and understand how it related to the childhood relationship I had with my mother. As boys, many of us couldn't be close to our mothers without losing ourselves in their needs, or without our energy being sucked out of us to sustain them. Or if our mothers were not there at all, then as adults our bodily hunger for closeness or distance may drive us and our partners crazy. Until we address our wounds in some way that brings us in touch with either our fear of being engulfed or our excessive need for physical contact, we will continue relating to other adults as scared little boys rather than as adults.

Here's another example of a son negotiating a rhythm of closeness with his mother, which was jeopardizing his relationship with his wife. You'll see how he can employ boundaries and limits to resolve the ongoing conflict that exists in his Mother-Son Dynamic. Wendell has been in recovery for quite some time now, but his mother and father haven't. Even though Wendell is forty-six years old, his mother's influence sticks to him like a spider's web. He realizes that his mother has been guilt-tripping him into doing her bidding for years, manipulating him to stay in contact with her. Some of her favorite sticky phrases: "Your father misses you. You should see him more often. He won't always be around, you know." "I haven't been feeling well lately. I always feel better when you come for a visit."

Often Wendell's mother places herself between him and his wife, Laurie. She gets him to side with her during arguments or to make choices in her favor regarding the smallest of things, such as where they should go for dinner. Laurie is thus furious about half the time they're all together, and Wendell's mother seems to thrive on upsetting her. Laurie has finally demanded that Wendell put her needs before his mother's maneuverings. This has made Wendell's mother come after him even more.

After much therapy and work in a men's group, Wendell has finally decided to break this cycle of addictive behavior, to alter rhythms he and his mother have unwittingly danced to over the years. He has decided that he must create boundaries strong enough to resist her barrage of guilt. Until he manages that, he doesn't want to see her for a while, but he's afraid to tell her this. He's still not completely convinced he has a genuine right to establish his personal rhythm of closeness with the woman who brought him into the world.

A hallmark of a healthy relationship is the freedom to choose how often to get together and how long to stay apart. The rhythm is defined by the needs of each individual adult. By using boundaries and limits, you can maintain your rhythm of closeness, respect your partner's rhythm of closeness, and keep the Mother-Son Dynamic from ruling your lives and loves. You can spend time together because both of you want to and not out of obligation or feeling you are held hostage until you meet their emotional demands.

As children we had to come to our parents when they called us or else we'd suffer the consequences. Today, when our mothers or fathers want us, many of us still feel like children, as though we would be breaking the rules if we didn't come when called. If, as adults, we still fear punishment by our parents, we have some deep work to do, especially if our parents are shaming, guilting, withdrawing from, or disowning us because we are trying to find our own rhythms of closeness.

If Wendell continues to be afraid of establishing a rhythm that works with his mother, he'll find it difficult to find his rhythm with others—particularly with his wife. He will move to other people's rhythms more often than his own, and he'll continue to stumble through life.

Exercise for Sons

How much space do we need? What is a healthy amount for us? Take a look at the pattern that was set in your childhood and answer the following questions.

- Was your mother too close to you? Not close enough?
- As a child, did you experience emotional incest? Remember the woman who tried to fulfill her loneliness and need for a partner with hugging and affection from her six-year-old son.
- Do certain physical actions your partner does trigger feelings that he or she is too far away or too close for comfort?
- Do you get anxious or even have separation anxiety in the present? In childhood, did your mother leave you when you were not expecting it, or when you needed her to be there with you?
- Would you like to try changing some things in your current relationship with your mother, such as how frequently you call or e-mail her, how often you visit her, and how much time you spend with her?
- Is there anything you would like to try changing with your wife, girlfriend, or partner in terms of the time you spend together?

Keep in mind that the goal of this exercise is to strengthen relationships by respecting your individual rhythms and not to escape or run away from your partner.

Exercise for Mothers

- Do you recognize yourself as a parent who may (even with the best of intentions) try to find fulfillment and affection from your son that should more appropriately be sought from another source, such as a partner?

- Do you have someone other than your son in your life to help meet social, affectionate, and even romantic needs?

- Have you ever said phrases regarding your child that sound like they could be said about an adult you were having a relationship with, such as "He makes a much better date than his father," or "To get a man this handsome to go out with me, I had to make him myself."

Exercise for Partners

- Are there times when you feel that your husband, boyfriend, or partner is pulling away? How do you react when he does this? Are you threatened by this?

- Do you take time for yourself and your needs and interests separate from your partner, and does he do the same?

MAINTAINING YOUR RHYTHMS

Members of a well-functioning family, group, community, or support network encourage one another to take their time and space, to connect when they're ready. They honor another's need to withdraw for a while in order to reevaluate his or her role in the relationship. A healthy mother might say something like, "I understand you need time away from me. I'll miss you, but take all the time and distance you need. Call when you're ready, and I'll be glad to talk if it's at a time that works for both of us. Until then, know that whether you're near or far away, I'll always love and respect you." At such moments, we are supported as we work through any fear of separation and we can freely speak our truth to mothers, fathers, or friends.

One thing I found out by living with Grace was how introverted I am and how much I required alone time and solitude to be creative and rested. Grace has a fraternal twin, and they were together 24/7 until adulthood. Plus, Grace's family has lots of cousins, relatives, and friends around quite a bit. I was more comfortable in the woods as early as eight years old, and about the only time we had company in my family was at parties, which included alcohol and wildness. My rhythms were very different from Grace's. I tried to honor my rhythms as best I could by taking extended periods away from her and from our daily life at home.

Back then I would say things like, "I'm in San Francisco now, and I'm going to stay here by myself a week until next week's event in Seattle."

"Oh, so that means you won't be home for this thing and that thing, and I won't get to see you for so long," Grace replied.

At first, this unsettled her, and it took us both some time and patience to adjust to each other's rhythms.

If you or a man you love grew up with the kind of mothering we have been discussing, he did not learn about boundaries and will have to learn as he grows. An important part of setting good boundaries is being able to stick with them and appropriately defend them when necessary. A few months ago I was teaching a workshop on "Boundaries and Limits." About three hours into the presentation, after hearing me say for the third or fourth time, "A boundary that can't be defended is not a real boundary but just a really good idea," Tom raised his hand and said, "I set good boundaries with my mother when I go to see her, but she refuses to acknowledge them. But it's not because I don't have them; she just ignores them."

"Then they're not really boundaries, because real boundaries can't be ignored. Think of the fence around your house. If you don't open the gate or tear down the fence or let your neighbor tear it down, they can't come into your space. Do you agree?" I said.

"No, I don't. Let me give you a personal example and you'll see what I mean. I set a boundary and she ignores it, and then I get very angry. Well, no, to be honest, I get enraged. See, I go over for dinner every Sunday. She's all alone now that my father is dead. We sit down and I put on my plate what I want and then she puts food on my plate that she wants me to eat, like brussels sprouts, which I hate. I tell her I don't want them and I don't want her to put food on my plate, that it's my plate!" He paused.

"So what happened?" one of the workshop participants said.

Tom continued. "She puts food on every time. I set a boundary and she ignores it every time, so it's not that I don't make boundaries clear."

"How old are you?" I asked this man, who owned an auto repair shop.

"I'll be thirty-two next month. What has that got to do with anything?" Irritation sharpened his voice. "What do you want me to do?" His face turned red with apparent anger. "Throw the food in her face? She's my mother, for Christ's sake."

"No, that would be rage, not defending a boundary."

Another workshop participant offered this suggestion. "How about saying something like 'Mom, if you keep putting food on my plate, I'm leaving.'"

From all the nodding in the room, I could tell most of the workshop participants liked that idea, but it wasn't the right choice either. "No, that's a threat," I said. There are many ways to set and defend boundaries without being abrasive or inappropriate.

Particularly in their own homes, mothers or fathers may feel they don't need to respect a child's boundaries. As Terry's mom, a single mother, told him when he was twelve: "This is my house, and as long as you live here I'll come into your room any time I want."

Most people I've worked with over the years who have boundary issues tend to think they can defend their boundaries only two ways. One is to leave the person who tends to ignore their boundaries, or do something like what Tom said, "Throw the food in her face," or some other violent or aggressive act.

So what would be a good way for Tom to defend his boundaries with his mother? Next time he speaks to her he could say, "Mom, I won't be coming home for Sunday dinner anymore. I'll be coming over on Sunday afternoon for tea only." Or, "Mom, I've already eaten, I'll sit here and watch you eat." If she asks him why not, he can answer, "When I'm eating with you I don't feel respected."

We have other options than just fight or flight, but Tom's vision was clouded, and obviously his issue with his mother was long-standing. Every time this man would visit his mother, the whole meal context would throw him into a regression, and, therefore, he could not think of how to handle the situation in a clear, adult manner. He regressed emotionally back to childhood because of the context he was in with his mother and having a meal at her house. In this regressed state he felt small, little, less than the adult he now is, and even reliving this scene in the workshop caused him to slip into a childlike state. Because he was regressed, he couldn't think clearly about some of the suggestions presented to him in the workshop; he could only think of fight (throwing food in his mother's face) or flight (walking out on her during the meal). (For more in-depth information on emotional regression, see my book *Growing Yourself Back Up: Understanding Emotional Regression*.)

HEALTHY AND FUNCTIONAL BOUNDARIES

Many authors and therapists tend to take for granted that every-one knows about boundaries, but I'm not going to do that here. I'd like to give you a further, fuller explanation of boundaries. Good boundaries actually increase intimacy, clarity, and communication and decrease verbal or emotional wounding, because you can say no when you need to. As children, saying no wasn't an option. As an adult, you can also say yes when you want to. You know where you stand, and this lets others know more about you. Knowing your boundaries enhances other people's feelings of safety and trust because they can rely on you when you say, "No more,"

"Enough," "Stop," or "It's okay; you can come closer." When we stay true to ourselves and don't compromise our boundaries and limits, no matter what others may think, everyone involved in the relationship wins in the long run.

A boundary is simply "This is how close you can come to me" in any area of life. This can be physical touch, emotional closeness, information closeness, financial closeness, and many other different ways. For example, you might not feel comfortable talking to your mother about your finances, so you draw a firm boundary around that whereas with your wife, the boundary would be closer in, if not completely disappearing at times. As an adult, you get to say when you need stronger boundaries or looser boundaries, and you can move them accordingly, based on the information you have about the person you're dealing with.

Most children who grew up in the '40s, '50s, and '60s, perhaps even the '70s, did not see boundaries put in place in a healthy and functional way. Instead, what most of us learned was how to erect walls due to the inability to create boundaries, and many of us are still confusing walls with boundaries. Here's the difference: boundaries create intimacy and can change with time and information. Walls are static, immovable, and stay put with time and information.

In my case, my informational boundaries were not respected, given that I didn't have any. So my mother would tell me things that were age inappropriate, and so even with all I know today about boundaries, I still have trouble when parents ask me what they should say to their children. Although I do give answers, they're not quick ones, because I have to stop and think for a minute what is appropriate versus what I experienced in my childhood.

The critical element of establishing your rhythm of closeness to anyone and everyone is first knowing what your boundaries are and also remembering that a boundary one cannot defend is not a boundary, but rather just therapeutic words or a good idea. It can be difficult to know right away where to establish your boundaries and determine what feels right to you, and that's okay. For example, you may think you can visit home for four hours at a time but discover that length of time is too long. Also, when you begin exercising and enforcing your boundaries, you may meet some resistance from those people in your life who are used to your not having these boundaries. Keep working toward what you need, and this will increase your chances of building stronger, healthier, adult-appropriate relationships.

SAYING NO—
A GREAT BOUNDARY WORD

If you don't desire to build walls that cannot be changed or moved, what do you do? You learn to say and mean the following words and statements that many people almost never say (and mean), or perhaps use only a few times in their lifetime:

No!
No More!
Enough!
Stop!

No is a complete sentence. The famous (or infamous) Gestalt therapist Fritz Perls said, "If you can't say 'No,' then your 'Yes' doesn't mean a damn thing." The person without boundaries is constantly playing the role of the yes man or woman, to the detriment of his or her physical, emotional, and spiritual well-being. Why is it so difficult to say, "Stop, I don't want to hear any more. No more! Enough!"? Because most people regress back to a time, usually childhood, where these words were not allowed, or our primary role models could not use them successfully without negative consequences.

Following are ways to stop and defend boundary violations, encroachments, and invasions:

- Identify the specific violation: "When you don't knock before coming into my room _____
_____."

- Tell the person how you feel not to have your space, needs, and feelings respected: "I get angry and scared _____
_____."

- Add energy, body language, and sterner words: "I'm serious about this," while putting up your hand in a stop motion or planting your feet firmly.

Know what you will and won't do should the violation continue or occur again. This is important for you to know, but it is also important that you don't tell the other adult. If you convey the consequences to them verbally, they will more often than not interpret your words as a threat or an ultimatum. (However, you should tell children what the consequences will be should they violate or disregard your boundaries so they can learn to make healthy choices in the future.)

Exercise for Sons

- With whom do you have good boundaries, poor boundaries, or no boundaries regarding physical touch?

- Perhaps you can answer this question honestly: Have you ever participated in a level of sexuality you were not comfortable with but did anyway?

- With whom do you have good boundaries, poor boundaries, or no boundaries regarding information that flows into you?

- With whom do you have good boundaries, poor boundaries, or no boundaries regarding your spirituality or religious beliefs?

- Did you have a parent or guardian who read your journal, rummaged through your chest of drawers or night table looking for evidence of bad behavior?

- Even when feeling uncomfortable, do you share information with your mother about things such as finances, business decisions, and your personal life?

- Do you feel obligated to share with your mother at her request any and all information?

- Do you listen to gossip, inappropriate, racist, or homophobic jokes or comments when you really don't want to?

Exercise for Mothers

- Do you practice boundaries with your son, whether he is a child, adolescent, or adult?

- Do you respect your son's privacy in age-appropriate ways?

- Do you set an example for your son by maintaining your boundaries (for example, taking time for yourself or not sharing with him information in your life that is not age-appropriate)?

- Take a look back at your childhood. Did your parents have boundaries with you as you were growing up? What kind of example or pattern did they set for you?

- Do you believe the example your parents set for you was healthy and beneficial to you as an adult? Do you wish they had done anything differently?

Exercise for Partners

- Do you practice boundaries with your husband or boy-friend? Name some examples.

- Do you have certain things you share with your female (or even male) friends that you should be sharing with your husband, boyfriend, or partner?

- Do you maintain areas of your life that were cultivated before your relationship with your husband, boyfriend, or partner? For example, if you regularly loved doing yoga before you entered this relationship, are you still doing it? If you set aside time for yourself to soak in a bath, do you still make time to do this? If you were an avid member of a book club, do you still participate? There can also be smaller things, such as if you love a certain food your partner hates, do you still find a time and a place to enjoy it yourself?

KNOW YOUR LIMITS

Limits are even more of a mystery than boundaries. Even professionals confuse boundaries with limits, if they discuss them with their clients at all. In a nutshell, a boundary says, "This is how close you can come to me." A limit is the emotional and intellectual knowledge of how far you'll go along with a situation, condition, marriage, job, parent, child, addiction, or behavior.

Many people have trouble knowing what their limits are both in personal and professional circumstances. Mildred, a compassionate and thoughtful mother who was overly active in her thirty-six-year-old son's life, called, very upset and angry. "I'm so angry with my son I don't know what to do," were the first words after "Hello." "I told him I would put him through two alcohol and drug treatment programs and then he's on his own."

"How is that going?" I asked.

"Not too well. That is why I'm so mad at him. I have now put him through four of the best and most expensive treatment centers in the country."

"Mildred, what were your limits?"

She fired back. "I said two. But obviously it wasn't. That's why I'm so angry."

"So you don't know your limits and you're angry with him because he doesn't know them either?"

Mildred laughed. "Oh!"

Setting limits can lead to a deeper connection with those we care about. When we don't know our limits, we go much further or stop short of where we want to be and how much we want to do with or for someone.

Not knowing our limits can turn us into caretakers instead of caregivers. Caregivers have good boundaries (and know their limits). Caretakers go way beyond where they really want to go. Unfortunately, caretakers often end up taking something out of those they are watching over—like their integrity, energy, self-esteem, or the money they find underneath the cushions on the couch or lying around. Many people who don't know their limits or don't pay attention to them tend to feel resentment and, therefore, need some kind of payment or restitution. In other words, we feel we have to take something for giving up something of ourselves that we do not want to give. People who know and respect their limits can care for others without resentment, without feeling like something is being taken from them, and as a result they feel energized by their giving to others.

As I said earlier, when we listen to our internal rhythms for closeness and separateness, we know what our limits are. If we stay true to our rhythms, we know how long we can visit our parents without falling into old, destructive conversations and patterns. If we know when to seek solitude to recharge our batteries, we won't have to push people away or run away from a relationship just because we can't say, "I need some time alone."

Another client of mine, Tony, was taking a sabbatical from interacting with his mother. I asked him, "When you resume your relationship, how long can you be with her before feeling overwhelmed?"

"Maybe thirty minutes before I'll become her little boy again, who stays much longer with his mommy, and we'll be in the same old dysfunctional drama we're always in."

"What would happen if staying thirty minutes or less became your limit?"

"We'd probably enjoy each other's company. I'd leave on a good note, because I'd still be an adult instead of a pissed-off kid who didn't want to ever come back and see his mother for a long time."

By seeing and articulating this payoff, Tony was able to set this boundary and keep his visits under his limit. His mother never really understood what Tony was going through, but she was fully aware that they were getting along better. Limits not only help us establish the difference between caring for and caretaking, they separate quantity from quality.

Love doesn't mean we have to let someone trample our boundaries. Quite the opposite. The stronger our boundaries, the greater the intimacy. Nor does it mean going to see our families when we really don't want to, for if we do, when we get there we're only partly present, and everyone will feel it. That's fear and guilt, not love. In contrast, the rhythm of love goes something like this: "I'm glad to see you and I bring all of me to you. I feel seen by you and heard by you and want to see and hear you, too."

Let's recap. Adult men and women can easily set boundaries and limits that, depending on the situations and people, can be pulled in, extended, or shifted based on choice, new information, or more experience. Our boundaries and limits should be clear to us and to those we love, live with, or work with. Good boundaries and limits help protect us without isolating people or pushing them away. They keep us at a safe distance so that we don't have to accept anyone's smothering, guilting, raging, shaming, abusive, or demeaning words, actions, or behaviors.

Exercise for Sons

- Can you identify times in your childhood when you went past your limits of comfort? As young children, we don't have the opportunity to set our own limits, but it is still valuable to see if and where these patterns were in our childhoods.

- As an adult, do you set (or try to set, or wish you could set) limits with your mother? Do you go past these limits and do more for her or spend more time with her than you would like?

- Are you able to set limits with other people? Are you able to enforce limits with others but not with your mother?

Exercise for Mothers

- Have you ever gone past your limits with your son when he was a child? For instance, did you threaten to reprimand him for certain behaviors but not follow through when he did them anyway?

- Have you gone past your limits with your adult son, like Mildred and her son in rehab?

- Have you in the past (and do you now) respect limits your son sets? Or do you feel because you are his mother that they do not apply to you?

- Write down some instances of when you went way past your limits with a lover, adult son or daughter, a parent, a relationship.

Exercise for Partners

Although you are not a direct participant in the Mother-Son Dynamic, you may be greatly affected by it. This is a good time for you to examine your own limits concerning your relationship to your partner and his mother.

Exercise for Sons, Mothers, and Partners

Following are a few more examples of less dramatic ways to think about limits:

- I'll be able to go only one more week.

- I'll explain this two more times.

- I can talk about this for thirty minutes.

- I'll give my boss one month to respond to my request.

Chapter 7

Growing and Knowing Ourselves, Free from the Mother-Son Dynamic

LOOK FOR YOUR OTHER HALF WHO WALKS ALWAYS NEXT
TO YOU AND TENDS TO BE WHAT YOU AREN'T.

—*Antonio Machado*

Now we've confronted the witch in our mothers, identi-
fied negative patterns we carried into adulthood, learned to express
our anger, and grieved what we didn't have (or had and didn't

want). We've learned that we need to find our internal rhythms and how to maintain those with limits and boundaries. As we continue to grow and have relationships with our partners, lovers, parents, and adult children based on ourselves and our rhythms, we will be able to more clearly see the witch that exists in us, whether we are sons, mothers, or wives and partners. And now we are at a point where we can learn to embrace it and let it become a part of our whole, conscious selves.

LIVING AND LOVING OUR INNER TWIN

Another way of thinking about the witch that hides in the forest of our unconsciousness is to understand that this darker self is our look-alike. Indeed, this self can pass as us in public whenever it feels like it. Like the witch, this double self—this doppelganger— must be embraced. The only way I am able to see the witch in my mother or wife is to see it loose and latent in myself. There's a lot of truth in that old AA saying, "If you spot it, you got it," or as the philosopher E. M. Cioran says, "Men's eyes see outwardly that which troubles them internally."

Popular culture has long dealt with the concept of the "evil twin." It's a frequent if clichéd plot device in movies and soap operas. Thomas Tryon's book *The Other* explored the theme as well. We are fascinated and frightened at the idea of someone who looks just like us but is our opposite in nature. Of course, the deeper meaning of these stories is that good and evil exist within each of us and that sometimes it's impossible to tell them apart.

I'd been thinking about this inner twin for some years before I met Grace. I was delighted when I learned that Grace is one of a pair of twins. When they were growing up, Grace said that her sister often drew more than half the attention—more than half of the hugs, the holding, and the comforting. But besides this real twin sister, Grace also has what I call an inner twin who figures prominently in our relationship and who goes wherever Grace goes. We all have this twin. I call mine Jack, my evil twin brother.

As I see it, this twin is the person who is more wounded than we are, the one who takes long walks when we sleep, who talks long after we should be silent, and who stays silent when we should be speaking our truth. It is that other self who dreams of adultery while we struggle to maintain our commitment to monogamy, the one who gives rein to forbidden desires. It's the other self who shows up when we're scared, threatened, or traumatized. This self is always ashen in color; its eyes are lackluster, and its shoulders sag toward the earth. When scared, this is the one who runs; when threatened, it's the one who fights for dear life; when traumatized, it's the one who dissociates and stares into space. This is the one who craves but is insatiable; who hates with a power that is more than human; who swears that life is unfair, unjust, unfaithful.

In our relationships, these twins play a major role. They live with us. Thus Grace, her Other, I, and my Other make a quartet, all trying to inhabit the same psychic and physical space. All couples live in this quaternary of quarrels, idiosyncrasies, lunacies, and inconveniences. And it is our partners' Others who, at the very least, disappoint us by being thoughtless, careless, and petty. It is the Other whom we divorce because of irreconcilable differences. It is this Other we sometimes feel the urge to kill, or who sometimes makes us feel like killing ourselves.

Grace's twin demands the same thing my Jack demands: attention, embracing, and even love. These twins are the side of ourselves our parents could not stand to see for fear of the questions it would raise about them and their ability as parents. It's the side we hid, fearing that if our parents became aware of it, they would leave us.

The way to begin loving your partner's Other is to let your Other out of the closet and let it roam through each room of the house, showing itself without shame. For me, the beginning point of this uncovering process was when I realized I had to show Jack to the world, specifically to Grace, and, more important, to myself. I needed to begin doing for myself what my parents could not do: live with and love this shadowy self. There is no way to love the lover's Other if we have little or no capacity to love our own. Somehow over my years with Grace, I've seen and shown more of the darker side of myself than in all the years before combined—especially the side that doesn't handle anger appropriately, even though I've written three books on the subject. And you know what? She lets it run wild like a desert pony. She has learned to embrace her Other self. Both women—the wounded one who wages war and the one who loves me, wounds and all—have stayed. And both of the "mes" love both of the "hers." Now, don't get me wrong. I don't believe I have to like Jack or to like my lover's Other self. But we do have to learn to go beyond toleration, a long way toward love, if the house we live in is to be less haunted by things unseen, unshown, and unspoken. Loving only one side of us is what our parents did, and we can't hold our lovers responsible for loving the side of us our parents ignored right away—certainly not until we ourselves learn to love it. But if we learn to, then we can hope our lovers can, too. If we don't, our houses, like the House of Usher in Edgar Allan Poe's short story "The Fall of the House of Usher," will be split down the middle and fall into an abyss.

This is where the quality of grace comes into a relationship. As I see it, grace is the gift that empowers us to do something that by ourselves we're not able to do. When we find our wounds and commit to healing them, rather than forcing our lovers to take responsibility for them, true grace descends. We then deepen our ability to be with another person. If we believe our partners are never going to become responsible for their own woundedness, then grace is the power that either points us in the direction of one who is willing to do this work or gives us the strength we need to live a solitary life. Through grace, the twin who has been with us in every relationship will be reconciled and integrated into our being. When that happens, our lovers automatically and unconsciously will begin to do what we've always wanted someone to do: love us, all of us, as we are, not unconditionally but maturely. Grace and I were just beginning this work. Our Others needed time, touch, and tenderness—first from ourselves and then from each other.

If you see pettiness, emptiness, jealousy, or greed in your mother or partner, you have it in you, maybe not to the same degree, but if you're honest, you'll admit it. Understand that your mother was a complex person with good and bad, and so is your partner, and so are you. You can show yourself and trust them to see all of you, and be willing to see all of them. Remember, she also came into the world with a shadowy twin whom no one approved. Says a character in Rachel Cush's novel *Outlive*, "'That is always a dangerous moment,' he said, 'to make a decision, when you're not sure what you deserve.'"

Exercise for Sons

The objective is to bring some of these hidden or shadow traits you possess into the light of day.

- Write down the personality or character traits your current or most recent partner displayed that made you uncomfortable. For example, do you feel your partner is too lackadaisical about time management, and does it frustrate you that she or he often runs late? Or do you feel your partner is too chatty and monopolizes other people's time?

- Write down your partner's personality traits you count as negative attributes. Could they actually also be traits that lie dormant in yourself (but you know are there) that he or she mirrors back to you?

- What are some positive things you see in your partner that drew you to him or her? Are these really just parts of you that you are longing to develop so you don't have to depend on your partner to provide them for you (since that's not her job, anyway)?

DEPART OR DEEPEN

When I am alone how close my friends are;
when I am with them how distant they are!
—Antonio Machado

Once we have freed ourselves from the confining roles we've adopted, once the truths are freed from the cages and caves of our bodies, we can go forward. Once we've stopped most of our dependency, discovered and articulated our rhythms of closeness and separation, and made friends with our inner witches, we have to ask ourselves: "To depart or deepen?" That is the question I must ask myself from time to time regarding my work, my family, my friends, and, most important, my partner in life.

By breaking the Mother-Son Dynamic, you'll have greater clarity of thought and feelings about coupling, context, and commitment. In other words, you'll have a greater connection to the voice inside you that can soothe you until you're calm enough to make clear, adult decisions.

Having mostly accomplished it myself and having helped lots of people do the same, it becomes very clear that if you can say goodbye to your mother as a boy and say hello to her as a man, you'll find letting go of almost anything or anybody much less challenging and less time-consuming. In other words, in direct proportion to how deeply you can let go of what might have been the alpha and omega of your existence and security, it becomes easier than you'll ever imagine to let go. This includes jobs, homes, friends, lovers, and even certain family members who no longer give, or maybe have never, you the support and compassion you've needed.

The bottom line here for deepening is that you may have looked outside yourself for a long time, with the mother having played the major role in soothing you, and now you have a greater ability to self-soothe: in other words, you'll stop looking for external remedies and comforts, whether that's people, places, or addictions, to reduce your anxiety when choosing either to stay or to leave a relationship or situation. Now you'll have the internal resources you can rely on more deeply for the rest of your life.

The first issue I had to deal with in my midlife self-examination was my work. As I separated from my mother's iron grasp, I had to decide for whom I was writing and leading workshops: her or me. After much introspection and fiery reflection, I decided that while these things may have been for her initially, they were now—and would henceforth have to be—for me.

Concerning my family, I had to decide whether to deepen my ties with them or do what I've always done—fly in and out of their lives, depending on my current level of anxiety. Some years before I had moved back to the South, partly as a way of deepening my connection to my sister and her daughter. Yet once I arrived, I found it difficult to connect, difficult to share the secrets and shame I'd felt toward my sister since childhood. The shame was about not being the loving brother she remembered and not being the rock-solid friend she needed me to be now as a man. As an uncle I felt I was faltering if not failing. So while we've visited with each other more in the last couple of years, we still really haven't seen each other. Still, my commitment to go deeper with her, to heal the wounds in our relationship, is greater than ever, as is my resolve to be a present uncle to my niece and a great-uncle to her daughter.

My decision to deepen my relationships to my closest friends came from seeing the incredible hole that was left once I'd left Austin and moved to North Carolina. It seemed I had to leave my southwestern home and go to my southeastern one in order to heal some old wounds I'd received there, not to mention the ones I'd inflicted on others and myself. After living anywhere for fifteen years, one is bound to create chasms between oneself and other people. Living on the farm for a year and a half, I felt those chasms had narrowed and transformed into small potholes that I could now avoid if I were careful. After a period of intense solitude provided by my rural setting, I realized that I sorely missed the old daily contact with my friends. Only by departing from that support network was I able to realize that community—my family of choice—was indeed a healing balm. We all should know this, but often we haven't allowed that balm to work its magic, largely due to the guarded way most of us have lived since childhood. In the bosom of the Blue Ridge Mountains, I had time to reflect. I saw that time spent in community and friendship is just as important as time spent in solitude in nature, that to give up one in favor of the other leaves us incomplete. I saw that a balance of solitude and community could make midlife manageable and the anticipation of old age acceptable, even ultimately enjoyable. Remember, one of the signs of passivity I mentioned previously is being out of balance. That applies to being alone and with others as well.

So I decided to return to my friends and family of choice by living in Austin for six to eight months of the year. I'd stay in North Carolina for the hottest part of the year, or whenever I needed to get away to write, walk in the mountains, or ride a horse.

I know such a scenario is not possible or even desirable for everyone, and that it may not always be financially possible for me either. But I also know that the feelings I have for my friends and for nature are so deep that I'll always need to find a way to embrace both and let both embrace me. The question I now faced was, do I deepen with or depart from Grace?

Twice during our most difficult times and once during our formal time of separation, I seriously considered flying, heading for the known instead of breaking the Mother-Son Dynamic. I thought about abandoning my resolve to work things out and just go back to the patterns that yielded little intimacy but a lot of intensity and drama: meet someone who falls in love with my persona and make her the repository for all my projections, the mirror for all my unfinished business from childhood. I could do what I've always done and keep getting what I've always gotten, which, as you know, is the definition of insanity. I'd meet someone who thought she knew who I was and I'd keep on trying to be that person, simultaneously trying to convince myself that she was who I wanted her to be: the partner who was also the mother and father who would love me unconditionally no matter what I did or said.

I realized during my grieving period and my separation from the mother I had (and from the one I never had) that infancy is the one period in life when we have the right to expect unconditional love from two people who could give it. When we are older, that time and those people are gone. Infancy will never come again. I hear so much sadness in those words as I string them together. But the truth, painful as it is, is also liberating.

I knew that, if I chose, I could depart and delve into a romance in which I'd reveal the same six or seven parts of myself I'd always shown to other lovers, the same roles I played for my mother. And my lover would show me the six or seven roles she'd played with her parents to please them. At this point in my life, though, it seems so much more important to find and show the other twenty, fifty, or thousand parts of ourselves that we ourselves may never have seen or shared.

A friend of mine, Bruce, is separating from his wife. He told me that he was leaving because he could not be himself with her. She wanted him to show only the parts of him she was familiar with and comfortable around. His fantasy, he said, was that another woman would allow him to show all those parts of himself that he couldn't share with his wife. As we talked, I realized it's easier to discover and reveal our hidden parts when we have a partner we can go deeper with, one who is also trying to discover her missing self, who seeks to integrate them into a whole person. Of course, as I've said, we can't heal each other's wounds. If we use our partners in that way, we'll just alienate them. What we can do is stay put and watch their hidden selves emerge, letting our hidden selves be seen in the process.

I realized during the first three months of my romance with Grace that I was showing more of myself to her than I'd ever shown to any woman. Typically during that phase I'd let out only the teacher, the pseudo-sensitive man, the die-hard romantic, the considerate soul applauded by mothers everywhere. Sure, Grace had seen those "acceptable" parts of me. She was also seeing the screamer, the silent one, the one who needs to sleep alone one night a week, the recovering control freak, the man who would rather be right than happy, and many of the other parts I had always been too afraid to show to any woman, particularly my mother, for fear it would scare her away.

Sometime in life a man gets into a canoe that isn't tethered to another, and he paddles out into the unknown: the real matrix of creativity, of ourselves. The Jungian scholar Helen Luke tells us, "The masculinity of the spirit is meaningless unless it enters into a feminine container, and ultimately no man can create anything without the equal participation of the woman without or within." Perhaps a partner waits on the other shore, surrounded by friends, where the mystery sleeps inside the unknown, waiting to be awakened, a surprise that can't be named. If a man lets go of his mother and stops seeking to be mothered by the woman he loves, he will find himself born into a new world every day and leave behind an old one every night. In the future, you'll be able to pick and choose, or be drawn to, people and relationships because of a freedom you've attained because you can trust yourself and others, perhaps even more than you could possibly ever trust your mother.

TO WANT ONE THING, OR VERY FEW THINGS

To live within limits, to want one thing,
or a very few things, very much and love them dearly,
cling to them, survey them from every angle,
become one with them, which is what makes
the poet, the artist, the human being.

—Henry David Thoreau

The desire for mother and for mothering causes suffering and blindness to the manifold forms that life has to offer. We want so much of what we should have had that we can't see what we've got. What I have right now is a beautiful day, the soothing sound of wind chimes, the sight of a horse rolling on its back in the grass, and a love close by.

We want, we want more, and we keep on wanting. I used to think that if I ever had all the things I have now, I'd yearn for nothing, and yet the hunger is still there; the yearning persists. What am I really longing for? One answer: a mother to bond with. But deeper than that, I wanted to let go of the desire for something I never really had. I had to stop clinging to a childhood that ceased to exist many years before. I had to feel every ounce of pain in my body that came as a result of that loss. According to the Buddha, the first noble truth is that "Life is suffering." The second is, "Desire causes suffering." And the third, "Cease to desire, and suffering will cease." I knew this was difficult but, at moments, possible. I have had moments in which I wanted nothing, not even the wind that was blowing or the air I was breathing. So absorbed was I in the blessing and grace of that moment that I let it mother me into and through the next moment. I knew that by letting myself go through the doorway of feeling, I could not only let my biological mother go, with the pain of not getting what I needed from her, I could, if I had to, let Grace go.

By gently and slowly letting go of desire, I can also let go of the fantasy that life, age, and the body don't have their limits. They do. There were days before we reached the age of—well, you fill in the blank—when life seemed infinite and daydreams and night dreams were equally probable. My mother told me when I was a small boy that I could do anything, be anything I wanted if I put my mind to it and worked very hard. I believed her message; it played in my brain for decades like a mantra: "I can do it. I can do it. I can do it." As we age, the body isn't able to do what it once could—drive eighteen hours with not much more in it than coffee and willpower. The metabolism slows down and the battle of the bulge increases and finally turns into a full-scale war. The hair turns gray, if it doesn't disappear altogether. The men with the most hair and the trimmest waistlines get the promotions. While I and many other men my age feel ten times better than we did in our twenties because we're not nearly so depressed, obsessed, and repressed, we are discovering that life comes with limits. We'll never pitch for the Braves, slam-dunk with Michael Jordan, or be millionaires.

There is something freeing about coming to terms with our limits. I'm free to be the best me that I can be.

It wasn't always so. For years I was a driven kind of guy. My mother remembers how, when I was two years old, my father brought home a tricycle for me, the first of the few gifts he ever gave me on his own. We lived in a part of town where there weren't any sidewalks, our driveway was gravel, and the street was too dangerous, so the only place to ride my new three-wheeled wonder was in the grass. Have you ever tried to ride a tricycle in tall grass? Damn near impossible. But at the age of three or thirty, we don't accept that anything is impossible.

My mother watched from the window while I pedaled as hard as my toddler legs could go, only to move a few inches before I fell over like the old man character in the 1960s show *Laugh-In*. Then I'd get back up again, determined to become a master tricycle rider, conqueror of the grass and weeds. After about four hours of this, my mother said that I finally fell off and just lay there. For a moment she thought I was dead. She came out, scooped me up, and discovered I was running a very high fever. That was the first time my "I can do it" attitude made me sick—it would not be the last.

When I was sixteen, I had my first mad crush on a girl, Penelope. She didn't love me. But I thought, "I can do it—I can make this sixteen-year-old, out-of-my-league majorette love me back if I just try hard enough, if I really want it." Of course, I couldn't. Nor could I make Laurel, my adult love, whom I wrote about in *The Flying Boy*, come back after she left me for the final time. I tried everything. I put my mind to it and worked very hard, but she was gone.

Once, at a wilderness therapy workshop, I decided to walk a wire over a creek. Nearly everyone who tried it failed, but I was determined to succeed. I managed to walk across without falling in, but I collapsed, exhausted, on the other side. I had worked so hard that I wore myself completely out; I probably ran a low-grade fever then, too. I felt no sense of victory—only relief. The objective of that "trust" exercise was to let go and to fall into the harness, trusting it and the folks yelling, "Let go!" Not me. I yelled back, "I'm going to do this!"

My good friend Caleb taught me how to play racquetball. During a recent furious game he walked over to me and touched my back very tenderly. "Relax," he said. "It's just a game. Enjoy it." As he spoke, I realized how tight I was. I understood then why I was completely exhausted after every game. I wasn't necessarily trying to win, just to play well, but I saw that I always worked my hardest, even when at play. Discovering this lifelong pattern made me sad. How much energy had I wasted over the years, trying to push my limits, trying to make things happen that didn't need to happen?

The other night I had a dream. I was in my first car, a beautiful burgundy 1961 convertible Chevrolet. The top was down and I was enjoying the feeling of limitlessness as I gazed into the sky. Suddenly I realized that I didn't know how to put up the top and latch it, and I became extremely sad. As I examine myself, I often still feel like a pimple-faced adolescent—no longer a boy, not quite a man, unable to go forward or backward in time. Often I've felt like regressing to the behavior that accompanies those adolescent years—driving around the block where an ex-girlfriend lives, calling her on the phone only to hang up. But I've realized I have limits to what I can do and become. As adults, even if we understand that we have many options, eventually we run out of time. We have to make choices: take some things, and leave other things behind. I no longer subscribe to the magical thinking that told me I'd always have limitless possibilities before me. At this point, my life is about many things, but one thing I know and feel for sure: it's about preparing to be born into the unknown, acknowledging limits, recognizing ceilings, and saying good-bye to some dreams and opening up to others. It's also about accepting the past as it was and weaving a present out of the good threads our parents gave us. It's about feeling our failures and finally forgiving and moving forward.

My mom was right to tell me that I could do anything and be anything I wanted to be. But she didn't go quite far enough. She didn't tell me to balance the energy spent working toward a goal with energy spent dancing with it and laughing at it. I didn't need to wear myself out trying to achieve something; rather, I could be open to letting it come to me. Young men have arms and backs strong enough to push that river for decades. But wiser men than I learn to stop pushing, to jump naked into that river, and to surrender to the current as it takes us to our ultimate destination.

Exercise for Sons, Mothers, and Partners

Write a letter to your younger, striving, anxious you. Tell him or her what you know now that you didn't know back then. Tell him or her that it's okay to slow down and take a deep breath. Read poet Mary Oliver's "You Don't Have to Be Good."

She says, "You don't have to crawl on your knees for a hundred miles through the desert repeating. You only have to let the soft animal of your body love what it loves."

Or perhaps before you turn sixty or seventy or thirty, your young self might feel the truth of this excerpt from Robert Bly's poem, "Things to Think."

When someone knocks on the door,
Think that he's about
To give you something large: tell you you're forgiven,
Or that it's not necessary to work all the time,
Or that it's been decided that if you lie down no one will die.

THE FIVE MOTHERS AND THE FIVE STAGES OF DREAMING

The Breeze at dawn has secrets to tell you.
Don't go back to sleep.

—Rumi

There are five directions: east, west, north, south, and in. As we'll discover when we are birthed out of the womb of our patterns, there are five mothers. They are the biological mother; the lovers we turn into mother; the adopted mother, Despair; and the Good Mother. Then the last mother, whom we almost always forget: the Moment as mother. Holding these five mothers in balance, we can discover how to dance with our lovers and wives, play with and parent our children, and be there for our friends.

When I reached the midpoint in my life, I saw I had achieved many of the dreams I'd had since childhood. I had a beautiful partner; I was writing books; I was living in a scenic mountain home. And I was closer to my friends and family than I'd thought possible a few years before. But while I'd realized many of my dreams, I found I was less able to inhabit them. I felt sad about this. In my grief, I started looking more deeply into the five mothers I am about to share. I began to understand how, in different ways, these mothers can nurture our ability to dream, to realize dreams, and to fully inhabit them—and so we also have the five stages of dreaming.

(I should caution that the five stages of dreaming, like the five mothers themselves, are merely metaphors that came in a waking, walking dream to this man. Don't try to make them fit you unless they feel true in your body or appear in your dreams.)

The biological mother brings us into the external world, out of the interior wonderland we have inhabited for nine months. This first mother meets most of our external needs (food, shelter) as well as some of our internal needs such as touch and mirroring. This mother's job is to make us as comfortable as possible with our external surroundings. She is our first social contact. How this mother was raised as an infant largely determines how freely she can give to her child. All too often, this mother gives the child only food for the body, leaving the soul undernourished—if not totally famished.

The biological mother produces a child who can dream or not, depending on the sanity of his childhood. The boy whose father is absent and whose mother tries to fulfill her needs through him is unable to see or dream just how wonderful he truly is. In the worst circumstances, where there is a great deal of abuse and neglect, he may not be able to dream at all. This abused boy may become the man who doesn't believe that dreams come true, who believes in nothing other than what he can see, feel, touch, eat, own, and control. This man cannot imagine a heaven because he grew up in hell.

The second mother, already discussed at great length in this book, is the lover we turn into a mother. This process can happen whether we're male or female. It begins with the dysfunctional relationship we had with our biological mothers. Due to lack of mirroring and touching, and having been wounded by abandonment, abuse, and neglect or smothering, we end up looking for the mother we needed in the faces of everyone we meet. Ironically, we are attracted to one who will wound us the same way our mothers did. After a struggle, such relationships usually end in disaster and divorce.

The second mother, the one we make of our lovers or partners, also affects our ability to dream. At this stage we dream that perhaps there may be someone out there in the world we can discover, court, and capture; someone who can end the depression the first mother helped create. Romance novels, movies, television, and popular music all echo our hopes for soul mates, "better halves," princes and princesses. Men and women who dream that "someday my prince/princess will come to rescue me" may hit bottom in their lives when their rescuers don't show up. These are the same people who, unable to satisfy their own dreams, are forced to accept secondhand ones, like the American dream of a family with 2.5 children, a house with a two-car garage, and a golden retriever. They lie awake at night longing for inner peace, worrying about how to pay for a dream they inherited rather than formed in their souls.

The third mother is the adopted mother, Despair. She is the mother who comes to us in adulthood when we discover we cannot change our partners into the perfect parent, either. We then let Despair mother us, stunt our spiritual growth and our creativity, before we are finally willing to embark on a mysterious inner journey that will take us into the depth and pain of our pasts so that we can begin to heal.

The third mother—Despair—is the mother of the third dreamer. This stage has a twist. For a while, the dreamer has the illusion that the love from his mother he longed for as a child has finally materialized in the face of his lover, his children, his credit cards, and his golden retriever. This illusion is always present during the honeymoon stage of relationships. For a brief time, he believes he has realized all his dreams. And yet around midlife he wakes up. He looks in the mirror and sees his father's face. He goes to sleep at night and dreams of more money, more fame, more of whatever he believes will make him feel better about getting up each morning and doing another day's worth of whatever he's done for years that has allowed him to purchase his dream. Don't tell this man he can't dream. He has his twenty-five-acre ranch in the country; he belongs to a prestigious country club and anticipates doubling his income next year. If this dreamer doesn't move to the next stage of dreaming, he'll become a sleepwalker, wandering aimlessly through his life, living out the second half of his existence in stylish emptiness. He'll get up every morning and take a dip in his pool, hoping to wash off the despair. He'll try to wash down his depression with martinis. At this stage, more expensive addictions often take hold—cocaine, sex, acquiring, gambling.

This process prepares us to receive and to appreciate the fourth mother in our lives, the one John Bowlby calls the Good Mother.

As I define it, the Good Mother is the energy produced by a nonsexual loving that comes from some unexpected person. At some point during our healing, we will need to find, feel, and be healed by this Good Mother. Says Dante about this woman, "When a man hears her voice, sweetness and thoughts of ways to serve others come into his body."

It is she who brings us feelings of safety, worthiness, and enthusiasm for living in the present as who we really are. The Good Mother may be anyone, man or woman, who increases our self-awareness and our self-understanding. She helps us accept ourselves more fully. Through her support and nurturance, we become less afraid of rejection or abandonment because she mirrors our radiance back to us, establishing in us a higher degree of self-worth. The Good Mother loves us. She is available to us as we heal. She listens and lets us speak our entire truth without judgment or without trying to fulfill her hidden agenda.

I have been fortunate in having experienced the Good Mother in the therapist I've been seeing for the last several years. Now, don't misunderstand me: I'm not saying my therapist is a Good Mother to me. No one can be this twenty-four hours a day; it is humanly impossible. I'm saying that in her I found and received the kind of energy the Good Mother provides. My therapist at the time was a woman who has human attributes and failings like anyone else, but through her I have come to know the Good Mother.

For years she was there for me every time I needed her—that's what a Good Mother does. She accepted me totally as I am and that, too, is what a Good Mother does. She didn't judge. She didn't begrudge. She didn't chastise or punish, though she would gently confront me—that's what a Good Mother does. She even allowed me to get angry with her on occasion and didn't need me to hold back or take care of her feelings; only a Good Mother can do that. And most important, she loved me through all my worst times and good times with the kind of love that demands nothing in return. She needed nothing from me. This is why it is not reasonable to expect a partner to be the Good Mother: partners need things from each other, and it should not be put upon them to give a needless love.

Cynics may find this hard to believe, but my therapist was not doing all this because of the money I was paying her. In my case, at least, she went far beyond the role of therapist. Does she do this for all her clients? She certainly means to. But it's likely that to some she didn't seem like a Good Mother at all. For me, though, she was. Until you have experienced this kind of love and nurturance for yourself, none of the words I write can convey what I have received. But I can tell you clearly that without it I would not be where I am at this moment.

Later on, I was also blessed with a male therapist who performed the same function and two or three very close male friends and a couple of female friends. It takes a whole community to raise one adult.

The Good Mother we always wanted, needed, and never had as a child can come to us even after our cribs are replaced by Tempur-Pedics and our heads are as bald as they were in our first days. This mother can feed our souls and make us more comfortable in our own skins. She can't wrap us in a blanket and bring us to her breast, but she can wrap us with a kind of love that our own mothers were unable to do because of their woundedness. The Good Mother can help us see that we're not the saints or the scum we were told we were, but merely human beings with feelings and flaws, all of us acceptable, lovable, and beautiful.

Look for her, find her, and let her love you. If she has good boundaries, you don't have to worry about loving her back or helping her or healing her. Don't try to be useful to her. Drink her in, let her help you, and depend on her. For God's sake, as soon as you can, trust her. Fall into her arms and trust that she will not leave. If she (or he) truly is a Good Mother, she can't abandon you—it's not in her nature. She will be there—not forever, but for as long as you need her. Find a Good Mother just once, and the healing spirit of this kind of love will be with you long after the flesh-and-blood mother has departed.

The fourth stage of dreaming is marked by an encounter with this fourth mother I've just described—the Good Mother. Experiencing even for a moment the kind of healing balm that comes when someone loves him just for himself, the dreamer is now able to inhabit his dreams. What's more, he can begin helping others inhabit their dreams. Like the Good Mother, this dreamer supports and nurtures the less experienced, younger seeker—the student, the child, the friend. Robert Bly calls the man who is able to do this in a loving, altruistic way a "male-mother." This dreamer will take concrete action to show others what the inhabiting of dreams looks like, sounds like, and feels like. This dreamer becomes a mature mentor, sharing rather than competing with younger or less experienced men and women. But this dreamer no longer wants to make "sacrifices" or even "contributions" the way he did when he was still unable to inhabit his dreams, when he was still putting himself last in order to take care of everyone else. Such a dreamer no longer needs to "make a contribution" at his soul's or body's expense in order to numb the despair he feels as he is finding that his dreams have all run dry. You see, self-sacrifice and forced contributions are often forms of rescuing and caretaking, and can be used to numb the pain of not being loved for who we are. If we feel loved for who we are, then our gifts and our ability to help are given with fewer strings attached, with few hidden agendas, but, though our gifts are fewer, they are more sacred because they come from a place of wanting to serve rather than sacrifice.

By experiencing and holding on to this deep physical and spiritual love, we will more fully be able to approach the fifth mother: the present Moment, the mother of all possibilities, the mother who constantly embraces us and lets us go, and who gives birth to us anew, in our wholeness and newness and longing, a million times each day.

If the dreamer embraces this Moment mother, or lets her embrace him, she will nurture in him his ability to fully inhabit his dream. Living in the present, in the Moment, cures the despair and depression that come from having lived in the past and the future for so long. This dreamer becomes aware that his partner is the dream come true, that his child is the dream in all its excellence. He joyfully celebrates having a home to contain his family, a place and enough time in which to celebrate their love for each other. This dreamer sees the sunset outside his window as if there were nothing else to see. He lets his dog lick his face because at that Moment there is only the love, the dog, the slurpy exuberance.

He looks at his wife of twenty years and understands that he has known only the woman she was, and that before him she is a mystery unfolding, as every day she becomes ever new in his eyes. In every Moment he falls in love with her over and over again. The woman he married is gone; so, too, is the past that produced them both. Even when it's time to pay the bills, he feels a momentary bliss in his ability to do so. This dreamer sees, as William Blake put it, "a world in a grain of sand and a heaven in a wild flower."

This man inhabits his dreams. He's living life moment by moment, thankful for the breath and the heartbeat, for the blood that carries him into the next moment of life. This man understands the old warrior's words, "Today is a good day to die." Someone who does not inhabit his dreams finds no good day to do anything and is certainly not content about the idea of death, for he knows in his heart that he has never really lived. But one who inhabits his dream is satisfied with who he is. He does not seek to become someone else. This man is willing to embrace himself as he finds himself. This doesn't mean that he stops working or wishing. It doesn't mean that his life doesn't continue to get better. It's just that he accepts his life on its own terms.

Reaching this stage, he is freer than he's ever been. This dreamer looks for people to spend time with who will accept him as he is. He, too, accepts them—flaws and all. He doesn't need to change them, to convert them, or to convince them that he should be loved as they find him.

This man is more interested in being—being a good husband, a good father, or a good friend—than in becoming a rock star, a millionaire, or a suffering poet. He finds new things to interest him, but his interest is on a different level than it was in his twenties. He is more likely to dance and play with his new endeavors as if they were games, and not be so concerned with mastering them. Some days he'll feel like he's leading the dance; other days he'll feel that his partner is leading him.

Exercise for Men

- To know where you are in the process I just described, the first step is to come out of denial about who your mother was and wasn't. I hope at this point in reading the book you have already taken this step, but you may want to make it more concrete by writing down words that describe your mother, remembering that taking her off the pedestal without demonizing her does not hurt anyone.

- The second step is to reclaim the mother projections you have put onto flesh-and-blood women, past or present. Make an honest list of who these women were or are and the ways in which you unintentionally, unconsciously tried to have them give you something or stop giving you something your mother gave or didn't. *If appropriate,* you may want to contact them and make sincere apologies, but if you think it would hurt them or someone they love, instead write down the apology and add a prayer for forgiveness; then keep it in your computer or burn it, but do not deliver it.

- The third step of this exercise is to acquaint yourself more fully with the despair that resides in you for not having listened and paid attention to your dreams and having accepted a much less satisfying dream that was not your own. Remember that grieving what was lost or never held in the first place is one of the exits out of despair (see Chapter 4). (Many other books are available on the subject of grieving, including *When Things Fall Apart* by Pema Chödrön, a Buddhist nun and one of the best teachers about grief.)

- The next step is to identify as clearly as you can who, either male or female, provided elements of the Good Mother. More often than not, this entails people who gave you something or tried to give you something with no strings or need for reciprocation. The giving was clean and driven by love or interest or compassion, not pragmatism or secondary gains. This could be accompanied by a note, e-mail, or letter (some people still write these) expressing your gratitude for those moments.

- The last step is to find what strategies, training, or teaching allows you to be in the present moment to everyone's benefit. For example, one of the most popular forms of achieving this in-the-moment awareness is called mindfulness. Much has been written about it, so I won't go into detail here, but it has helped me and many of my clients and students. For those of you in recovery or who want to be, the twelve-step programs of Alcoholics Anonymous, Narcotics Anonymous, and Al-Anon encourage practicing being in the day fully, with the goal of being fully in the moment. Christian contemplation and Christian meditation will be useful to many, as will yoga, creativity, tai chi, and certain forms of therapy.

THE MYSTERIOUS OTHER

And I have been circling for a thousand years,
and I still don't know if I am a falcon,
or a storm, or a great song.

—Rilke

By the Other (not to be confused with the twin, or the other side of you) I don't just mean other people. The Other is everything other than oneself—sky, earth, sun, moon, myriad beings, myriad things. The mother we never had is also this mysterious Other, and we go in search of her. As one woman said to me once, "Drop the *M* from *Mother* and what you get is the 'other.'"

The Other is everything we think and feel we've lost since childhood. The other is all that we desire, all that pulls us with magnetic allure because we feel the lack of it. If all we've had for a long time is darkness, then sunlight is the Other. When we've lived our lives according to what is practical for so long, then whatever is whimsical is the Other. When we've been in our heads too long, the body is the Other: we see a beautiful body and want to merge with it, not just sexually, but wholly, even obsessively.

Most of us put our faith and trust in that which is not Other. For example, if we're used to darkness, we trust darkness and regard light with suspicion. And, while we may be tired of living in our heads, the thought of living anywhere else terrifies us.

All of life pulls us toward this Other. I am not a patient man, and so naturally I am constantly confronted with long checkout lines and inefficient clerks to learn patience—my Other. Those who can't sleep anywhere but in their own beds are almost always in relationships with people who can sleep anywhere, anytime, even when they're not particularly sleepy. The body we depend on gives out, so we have to discover our minds. Our money runs out and we step—or are pushed—into the Mystery of poverty to understand that we are more than the accumulation of our wealth. A widower becomes comfortable with solitude, only to meet a wonderful companion who wants to share his life. The boy who longs for a relationship with a girlfriend he has lost is in a good position to discover something feminine inside himself that he will never lose. On a brighter note, one person in the relationship always knows where the car keys are; the other person doesn't even know where the car is. No two people sharing a bed, a life, or a season want the windows closed at the same time or the thermostat at the same temperature.

It might seem that when we date and marry we are embracing the mysterious Other. But usually we're really not. Instead of recognizing and honoring our "significant others," most of us begin trying to change them from the unknown into the known as soon as the proverbial honeymoon is over. According to the old joke, we bring each other to the altar so that we can begin to alter each other.

For example, typically the man tries to get the woman to talk and relate to the world in the same way he does. He may do this though trickery, manipulation, coercion, sweet talk, or even abuse, telling her that her way is not good enough. And many women do the same thing. They try in any way they can, sometimes subtly, sometimes overtly, to get their spouses to be as spontaneous, as orderly, or as worried as they are.

It usually takes several years—even a lifetime—before we give up, stop pushing the river, and accept each other as we are. But often, before this happens, we experience withdrawal, despair, depression, and frustration because we haven't been able to shape another human being into our own image. The ritual of dating, as practiced in contemporary Western society, is one of two times I am aware of when we are most willing to appreciate the beauty of the other. This is partly because in the early stages of a relationship, the real man or woman has not yet fully emerged to threaten our customary way of being. (A Southern man will lie and say he has been to the ballet in this stage of romance.) We can afford to be fascinated with the people we date because early on we can usually manage to hold on to our personalities and our personal power. We know that should we choose to do so, we can go back to our own homes when the evening is over. We can conveniently lose their phone numbers and never call again, if that's what we choose to do.

The other time we fully appreciate the Mystery of the Other is when a relationship ends through separation or death. At these times it's easiest to remember what it was we cherished about the Other, especially the differences. We recall how what we liked in them was what we longed for, and, rather than finding it in ourselves, we let them carry it for us right into the divorce court or into the coffin and out of sight.

This is the essential nature of this Mysterious Other—it's always disappearing from view. The sun is always replaced by the moon. Spontaneity is there and then it, too, is gone. Discipline: now you see it, now you don't. The Buddhists have a word for this coming and going: *Tathagata*, a Sanskrit word that literally means, "Looks like it's going, looks like it's coming." We can recognize the Other when it comes, because that Other is already in us. We see it going for the same reason. Our biological mothers are our "First Other." With the help of healthy mothering we learn to differentiate ourselves from our biological mothers somewhere around the age of eight to twelve months. But when the mothering we receive is unhealthy, we keep seeking a loving Other for the rest of our lives. All the while we are unaware that She or He is, in fact, present within us, continually, until the day we die.

That girl we met and loved at sixteen, who appeared in our dreams until we were thirty-three, the great Other of our youth, is still present in our bones and being. She has never left. She was in us all along, or we would never have recognized or wanted her in the first place. Rumi says, "The minute I heard my first love poem I went looking for you. Lovers don't find each other; they've been in each other all along."

I cannot count the number of men I've worked with over the last thirty years who have a "first love," "love of my life," or "soul mate" who haunts them some every day and every restless night. They are often married but still carry some gift she gave them or look at photos of her from long ago.

The Other only seems so frighteningly mysterious and ultimately so desirable because, even though it's been in us all along, it's unrecognized, undernourished, ignored, unclaimed. The Other lives in our unconscious, in that part of our inner world that C.G. Jung called the shadow:

> The shadow is a tight passage, a narrow door whose painful construction no one is spared who goes down to the deep well. . . .
> For what comes after the door is, surprisingly enough, a boundless expanse full of unprecedented uncertainty, with apparently no inside and no outside, no above and no below, no here and no there, the mine and no thine, no good and no bad . . . it is where the soul

of everything living begins; where I am indivisible this AND that; where I experience the other in myself and the other-than-myself experiences me.

If the burning bush had not been inside Moses all along, he'd never have seen it. If your wife had not been in you all along, she would have walked right by you, maybe even bumped into you at that party where you met, but you wouldn't have seen or felt her. You might have thought it was only a rude wind or vertigo that made you stumble; instead, you fell in love.

The Mystery of the Other awaits us all. It enlivens us, keeps us from being bored, motivates us toward wholeness, teaches us, hurts us, connects us, consecrates us. It makes us less needy and more conscious and loving. The more we find the Other within ourselves and the more we bring our own Other out of the shadows and into the light, the more enthusiastically we appreciate and enjoy another person's Otherness.

GOING FORTH

We must somehow take the wider view,
look at the whole landscape, really see it,
and describe what's going on here.

—Annie Dillard, *Pilgrim at Tinker Creek*

It was a few days after Easter. Flowers were in bloom and Austin was cool, unlike the months that were soon to follow. It was the day Grace and I decided it was time to part "forever." The first twenty-four hours after she left, I felt good, full of hope. I thought, "Now we have the greatest possibility of putting our relationship back on track because we've stopped the dysfunctional dance. We've stopped stepping on each other's toes and souls." I told my friend Bill, "Grace is sure to see that we've broken the gridlock. Then she'll be back and we'll work it out."

The next day I woke up and looked my fantasy in the face. I thought, "My God, she's not coming back."

Then the day after that, I woke up and looked reality in the face and thought, "My God, I don't know what's going to happen."

I realized I couldn't control or predict either my behavior or hers. I might go to her and ask her to come back; then again, I might not. She might return in two minutes, or she might never return. And I realized that even if she did come back, I had no guarantee that she—or I—would stay together.

For several days I dwelt in a darkened tomb I made out of worry, fear, and fantasy, trying to get control of the uncontrollable. Finally, I rose from the deathbed of this relationship. I showered, shaved, and walked out my self-imposed isolation. It was as though I had risen, if not from death, then certainly out of a very long and deep sleep. Opening my eyes and my heart, I saw that not only was I unable to predict what another human being would do but I actually felt better when I didn't try. In this, the Moment, I was ready to inhabit the Mystery in my relationship to Grace as well as in other parts of my life. When I admitted to myself that I didn't know what was going to happen, my fear lifted and I was left with hope.

To my infinite relief and joy, Grace came back a few days later and we talked about the patterns, the pain, and the possibility of taking our relationship one day at a time. We finally decided to go our separate ways. We decided to let the Moment mother us both into being gentler with ourselves and each other than we'd been.

Will we ever get back together permanently? And if we do, will we part again? I don't know. Will anything in this book I've written help anybody? I just don't know. All I know is I can love her, myself, others, and God better and more deeply than I once could.

But I'll tell you why I'm ending the book this way. First, I've been praying and working to learn how to let go and let real grace move me from one moment to the next. I want to step into the unknown and uncontrollable as fully as I possibly can at this point in my life. I've had some success doing this in my work, and I feel freer than ever in a profession I almost walked away from simply because I was so tired of trying to control and predict so I could avoid failure in the future. I wanted the same kind of freedom as a child growing up—the freedom to be me, freedom from worry, stress, and control. I wanted the freedom that comes from being in the moment, one of the hardest things for me to do. I wanted the freedom that comes when we finally accept that we don't know what is going to happen, who is going to live, who is going to die, whose marriage will last, whose won't, who will come, who will leave, who will come back.

I wanted to enter this unknown place with the woman I call Grace, but not only her. And just as I've gotten healthy enough over the years to stop trying to change you, my audience, and let you be who you are, I wanted to be able to do this with Grace. Even after years of recovery and therapy and teaching thousands of people and writing over twenty books, I still struggle to hold on to the illusion of control. Grace and I continue to heal our childhood wounds, learning to take more responsibility for our lives. Every day we learn more about forgiveness and love and feel better and better all the time. Yes, we are friends. While we no longer live under the same roof, she will always be part of my family of choice.

Still the Mystery encompasses me. What the next movement, or the next moment, holds is as mysterious to me as Mars, motherhood, or masculinity. And having worked so hard, I'm at last feeling ready to forgive my biological mother completely, knowing with my whole body, soul, and brain that she did the best she could do. Most of the time I have one foot in and one out. When I get both feet in, you'll hardly recognize me: I'll be easier to be with, less aggressive, less angry, more nurturing, gentler, stronger. I won't take myself, my little victories or setbacks so seriously. I'll get up at 3:00 AM to work if I want to, wear double-knit pants if they're comfortable, and eat chocolate without fearing that I'll bring a halt to Western civilization. I'll laugh more, let more love in.

What about you? Are you going to let go and stop wanting the mother you never had? Are you going to let go of the Ghost Mother you had? Is it time to stop turning lovers, wives, and aging, still-living mothers into mothers? Mother, will you let your grown son go so he can live his life and loves as the separate adult, now your equal, that he is? Wives and partners, will you do your own work and take a clear look at how you relate to your man and his mother?

May I suggest that you not rush this or hurry the process? An old Arab proverb says, "Haste is of the devil; slowness is of God." Be gentle with yourself and others as you grow up, grow old, and learn to love anew every day for the rest of your life.

A Final Note

Some of the words you've just read I wrote some time ago, and others I wrote just days ago. So much has changed, especially my mother, my father, and me. Now when I call my parents, my mother talks to me for a few minutes and then warmly says, "Here's your dad. I know you want to talk to him. I love you. Hope to see you soon, but you take care and come and see us when you can."

Who is that woman? Certainly not the mother I grew up talking and listening to for hours on end. Several months ago I went for a visit, and I'll never forget this scene. My eighty-four-year-old father was building something and was using a power saw, whirring away as I got out of the car. As soon as he saw it was me, he flipped the off switch. We hugged and he said, "Come on in and let's talk a while."

My mother was in the dining room, painting the staircase. Without so much as putting her brush down so as not to miss a stroke, she hugged me with one arm and kept right on painting. Who is this father who never stopped anything to greet me, and this woman who would have stopped the earth spinning on its axis to visit with me when I came home?

What happened to Grace? Before we said good-bye I was speaking at a recovery conference at William and Mary in Virginia. There I picked up a brochure detailing a master's program in counseling. Long story short, she and her daughter moved to Virginia. Grace earned her degree and has become one of the best therapists in the Southeast. She loves her work, her recovery, and the man she's been with for years. We are still very close and have been the best of friends. Her daughter, my unofficial stepdaughter, attended my wedding to Susan, whom I'll tell you about in great detail in my next book.

Where do I go now? What do I do next? This man who took decades to stop sonning and is no longer by any stretch a mama's boy and who almost never, I say almost never, turns women into mothers? On the next part of the journey, on to the next book, on to the rest of my life.

Thank you for joining me on one of the most important legs of my journey. I hope it has been helpful. If it has, let me know. I'd love to hear your story.

Postscript

Dear Ghost Mother (you at age twenty, thirty, or forty)
and Dear, Dear Mother (at eighty-two):

I have spoken my truth for the first time ever regarding our complex, complicated relationship. It took me many years, decades even, to go there and write about what it was like with both of you, the Ghost and the human.

I hope this book will help shorten for others the journey we took to become friends and equals. Here are a few more truths that didn't get into the body of the manuscript but did get into my body and soul:

- You taught me to love words and so I became a writer.
- You taught me to love books by reading to me at an early age. You have seen my extensive library. When I say I'm ready now to party, that means I'm ready to read a good book!
- You instilled in me a love of God in a way only you could, and what a blessing.
- You (and Dad) gave me a pretty damn good sense of humor.

- You gave me an antiracist view of the world by the time I was in kindergarten, which I'll always be grateful for but never understand, given our Southern hillbilly background.
- You gave me the gift of letting go as your son so I could finally have a man-to-man relationship with my then-estranged father.

So you see, it is not black or white, good or evil. It's all human, and the following poem sums it all up in better words than I'll ever produce this lifetime. I dedicate this poem by Antonio Machado to all the mothers, sons, lovers, and wives:

Last Night As I Was Sleeping

Last night as I was sleeping,
I dreamt—marvelous error!—
that a spring was breaking
out in my heart.
I said: Along which secret aqueduct,
Oh water, are you coming to me,
water of a new life
that I have never drunk?

Last night as I was sleeping,
I dreamt—marvelous error!—
that I had a beehive
here inside my heart.
And the golden bees
were making white combs

and sweet honey
from my old failures.

Last night as I was sleeping,
I dreamt—marvelous error!—
that a fiery sun was giving
light inside my heart.
It was fiery because I felt
warmth as from a hearth,
and sun because it gave light
and brought tears to my eyes.

Last night as I slept,
I dreamt—marvelous error!—
that it was God I had
here inside my heart.

—translated from Spanish by Robert Bly

About the Author

For thirty years, JOHN LEE has been guiding lives and relationships through addiction, recovery, emotional ruin, rage, grief, and desperation, and into new strength, hope, functionality and fulfillment. He wrote the bestseller *The Flying Boy*, as well as twenty other healing books, and he has been featured on *Oprah, 20/20, The View,* CNN, PBS, and NPR. He has been interviewed by *Newsweek, The New York Times, The Los Angeles Times,* and dozens of other national magazines and radio talk shows. John earned his master's degree at the University of Alabama, where he taught English and American Studies. At the University of Texas, he worked on his doctorate, and he taught Religious Studies and Humanities at Austin Community College. He is founder and former director of the Austin Men's Center, where he ran men's groups and sessions for individuals and couples. Along with poet Robert Bly and others, John became a recognized leader in the men's movement and is an early pioneer in the field of recovery and addictions—he has keynoted hundreds of clinical conferences around the world. He lives in Mentone, Alabama, and Austin, Texas.

Sources

Beattie, Melody. *Codependent No More: How to Stop Controlling Others and Start Caring for Yourself,* Hazelden, 1992.

Bly, Robert. *Iron John: A Book About Men,* Da Capo Press, 2004.

Bly, Robert, James Hillman, and Michael Meade. *Rag and Bone Shop of the Heart: Poems for Men,* Harper Perennial, 1993.

Chödrön, Pema. *When Things Fall Apart: Heart Advice for Difficult Times,* Shambhala Classics, 2000.

Johnson, Robert. *He: Understanding Masculine Psychology,* Perennial Library, 1989.

Jung, Carl. *Memories, Dreams, and Reflections,* Vintage, 1989.

Keen, Sam. *Fire in the Belly: On Being a Man,* Bantam, 1992.

Love, Patricia. *The Emotional Incest Syndrome: What to Do When a Parent's Love Rules Your Life,* Bantam, 1991.

Luke, Helen. *Old Age,* Lindisfarne Books, 2010.

Mellody, Pia. *Facing Love Addiction: Giving Yourself the Power to Change the Way You Love,* Harper One, 2003.

Tryon, Thomas. *The Other,* New York Review of Books Classics, 2012.

Index